REBUILDING PITTSBURGH

REBUILDING PITTSBURGH
RIDC and the Transformation of the Steel City

JEFFERY FRASER
EDITED BY DOUGLAS HEUCK

Globe
Pequot

Essex, Connecticut

Globe
Pequot

An imprint of The Globe Pequot Publishing Group, Inc.
64 South Main Street
Essex, CT 06426
www.globepequot.com

Distributed by NATIONAL BOOK NETWORK

British Library Cataloguing in Publication Information available

Library of Congress Cataloging-in-Publication Data available

ISBN 9781493091423 (paperback) | ISBN 9781493091430 (ebook)

Contents

Introduction

There they were in Pittsburgh's David L. Lawrence Convention Center, having gathered for their annual summit: U.S. president Barack Obama, French president Nicholas Sarkozy, German prime minister Angela Merkel, Italian prime minister Silvio Berlusconi, British prime minister Gordon Brown, and other leaders of the Group of 20 nations. The world was only weeks removed from the end of the worst economic recession since the Great Depression and struggling to recover when the three-day summit opened on September 22, 2009. In the eyes of the U.S. president, the experience of economic calamity and uncertain recovery that each nation shared made Pittsburgh the "perfect venue" for the discussions among the global economic powers that were to follow.[1] Pittsburgh and the surrounding southwestern Pennsylvania region had been forced down that hard road fewer than three decades earlier. Yet, on that comfortable autumn day, the city with its clean and busy downtown, reclaimed riverfronts, and redeveloped brownfields nurturing high-tech start-ups was the picture of economic health.

"This city has known its share of hard times, as older industries like steel could no longer sustain growth," Obama explained to the G20 dignitaries. "But Pittsburgh picked itself up, and it dusted itself off, and is making the transition to job-creating industries of the future. It serves as a model for turning the page to a 21st century economy, and a reminder that the key to our future prosperity lies not just in New York or Los Angeles or Washington—but in places like Pittsburgh."[2]

The image of Pittsburgh as a shining example of rebirth after industrial decline captivated the nearly 4,000 national and international journalists on hand to cover the G20 summit. "Slowly, Pittsburgh's transformation has captured the attention of other communities now confronted with economic crises of their own," wrote the *Financial Times* of London. "This week's Group of 20 Summit will only highlight the city's progress, signaling to cities such as Detroit and Cleveland that they can once again become vibrant."[3] *The Atlantic* reported: "If Angela Merkel, Silvio Berlusconi, Gordon Brown, or any of the other hundreds of foreign government officials are looking for inspiration on how to revive their economies, they could do worse than to walk through Pittsburgh's neighborhoods, which brim with reminders that just about everything old can be new again."[4] Writing in *Forbes*, Raquel Laneri described Pittsburgh as "the new symbol of modernity and progress."[5]

Few regions had endured the scale of economic disruption that southwestern Pennsylvania experienced in the 1980s and managed to rebound in ways that earned such accolades. Steel and other durable goods manufacturing upon which the regional economy had heavily depended collapsed. Most of the region's nearly two dozen steelworks that had fed the building of America for longer than a century were shuttered in rapid succession. More than 150,000 manufacturing jobs disappeared. Unemployment rivaled the jobless rates the United States experienced during the Great Depression. Nearly 300,000 residents fled the region, mostly young adults in search of job opportunities. Several mill towns that lost manufacturing saw their tax revenues dwindle to less than what was needed to cover the cost of public services and infrastructure.

Recovery was not painless nor was it as complete as the breathless reviews from out-of-town journalists covering the G20 summit suggested. The exodus of residents was stanched, but the region's population never returned to pre-industrial-decline numbers. Although unemployment stabilized, job growth remained mostly tepid. Municipalities hit hardest by the loss of industry struggled to attract new investment and avoid becoming pockets of poverty, vacancy, and blight. Several defaulted and fell into state receivership.

But southwestern Pennsylvania emerged from crisis with an economy that was far more diversified, with strengths in the fields of education, health care, and technology that were poised to redefine the global economy. No longer did the region rely on primary metals, mining, and manufacturing as its chief source of jobs and wealth. By the dawn of the 21st century, health care was the region's largest employer. More people worked in education than in manufacturing. And within the manufacturing sector itself, those who made electronic equipment and instruments outnumbered those who worked in the few remaining steel mills. The City of Pittsburgh underwent a makeover. Downtown residency slowly gained popularity. A decades-long effort to rid the city's riverfronts of commercial blight transformed them into public parks and bike trails. One by one, the rusting hulks of abandoned steel mills and retired factories disappeared from the region's river valleys as the brownfields they left behind were reclaimed, reimagined, and rebuilt as homes for new institutes, research labs, and companies, many focused on exploiting the potential of new technologies. Hope and a brighter outlook for the future gradually replaced the gloom that had weighed on the region.

Southwestern Pennsylvania held several advantages that enabled it to become the poster child of Rust Belt Renaissance. Among them was the willingness of business leaders, government officials, heads of the region's well-endowed philanthropic foundations, and its accomplished universities to collaborate on solving complex problems, raising money, and putting plans in action. They had done it before, when near the end of the Second World War, a burst of civic-minded cooperation bridged partisan divides to tackle air pollution, flood control, urban redevelopment, and other issues that threatened future growth and prosperity. In the wake of industrial decline in the 1980s, the coalition added a powerful new partner: the region's major research universities. Together they took inventory of the region's strengths, worked out strategies to capitalize on them, and found the money and political influence to bring them to bear on turning around the fortunes of southwestern Pennsylvania.

Strategies focused on exploiting another advantage—a legacy of research and innovation. The region had long been a center of innovation with industry-changing ideas flowing from major corporate residents, including Westinghouse, United States Steel, the Aluminum Company of America, Heinz, Gulf Oil, Pittsburgh Plate Glass, and Koppers. As those traditional industries weakened, the universities emerged as the leading source of innovation. Importantly, they recognized their potential to influence the regional economy. The University of Pittsburgh Medical Center became the dominant health care network in the region and a leading employer. Between them, the University of Pittsburgh and Carnegie Mellon University built world-class programs in biotechnology, artificial intelligence, software, robotics, and other fields on the cusp of reshaping the global economy. They were among the most influential of what the late University of Pittsburgh professor of history and social work, Roy Lubove, described as a "new breed of entrepreneurial, development-oriented nonprofits"[6] that coalesced around modernizing the Pittsburgh area economy.

This is the story of perhaps the least-known of those nonprofits, a small economic development organization that has played an outsized role in reshaping the southwestern Pennsylvania economy over the course of eight decades. The Regional Industrial Development Corporation was established in 1955 by the powerful civic leaders behind Pittsburgh's so-called Renaissance I. It was assigned an ambitious mission: diversify the economic base, attract new companies, encourage existing ones to expand, create jobs, and improve the quality of life of residents to ease mounting concern that the region had come to rely too heavily on its steel and manufacturing industries, which were beginning to show signs of weakness.

RIDC was allocated no money to pursue its mission, surviving instead on contributions from members of its board of directors, which included the region's largest companies. The nonprofit spent its first few years conducting economic research, but it struggled to find a way to attract and nurture businesses and keep them from leaving. It wasn't until its charter was amended to allow it to buy land, build on it, and otherwise operate as a commercial real estate developer that RIDC found an approach to fulfilling its mission that worked. Finding homes for new, expanding, or relocating companies had long been a challenge. Industrial Pittsburgh had been built to the specifications of big manufacturing with its sprawling mills and plants, each of which was spread over hundreds of acres. Ready and affordable real estate for small-to-mid-sized companies, research labs, and start-ups was in short supply—particularly highly coveted square footage in and around the crowded university corridor that runs through Pittsburgh's Oakland neighborhood. While shuttered industrial sites suddenly opened up plenty of space, much of the acreage stood as contaminated brownfields unsuitable for most other tenants. Such sites attracted little interest from private developers, whose need to realize a profit on their investment sooner rather than later ran counter to the realities of flipping brownfields whose environmental cleanup alone was difficult and costly, and prospects for growth in the depressed mill towns where they were located were uncertain.

As a nonprofit economic development agency, RIDC had the advantage of "patient money" to invest, and, during its early years, had access to state grants and low-interest loans that private developers didn't. Its leadership, almost to a man, pursued the nonprofit's mission with a high tolerance for risk. The nonprofit was a pioneer in developing industrial parks in the region, building its early business campuses on underused acreage in the Pittsburgh suburbs, which became popular among new companies and expansion-minded established companies as well. It learned to design buildings with the flexibility to accommodate a range of tenants and to cobble together public and private sources of capital into financing packages that kept rents affordable, often below market rates. It became adept at imagining and demonstrating markets in places where others had yet to see them. Revenue from RIDC's suburban parks eventually enabled it to become financially self-sufficient—a milestone that was challenged during the dark days of industrial decline, when local and state governments turned to the nonprofit to undertake the difficult and expensive redevelopment of abandoned steelworks and factories for desperately needed new employers. From its earliest days, RIDC recognized the scientific and medical innovation nesting in the universities as a largely untapped economic resource, developed relationships with the schools, and became their developer of choice building research centers and labs that would draw some of the biggest names in technology to Pittsburgh, including Google and Apple.

The G20 delegates in 2009 had only to travel four miles up the Allegheny River from their gathering at the convention center to see RIDC's fingerprints on the region's recovery. Seven years earlier, it had acquired an abandoned steel mill, a vacant chocolate factory, and other neglected parcels in Pittsburgh's Lawrenceville neighborhood and redeveloped them as research, manufacturing, and business-incubator space. The properties and their neighbor, Carnegie Mellon University's National Robotics Engineering Center, became the epicenter of a fast-growing cluster of artificial intelligence, robotics, and autonomous systems companies and entrepreneurs—referred to locally as "Robotics Row"—that would attract billions of investors' dollars and national attention. South of the city, RIDC's work could be seen in the cities of McKeesport and Duquesne, where it built industrial parks from the ruins of two shuttered steelworks in the Monongahela River valley. East of the city was Keystone Commons, a campus of small-to-medium-sized companies developed from what had been the historic Westinghouse Electric & Manufacturing Company's East Pittsburgh works, which more than a century earlier manufactured the transformers, generators, and other equipment that electrified America. More evidence of RIDC's role in the southwestern Pennsylvania economy would be apparent in later years, including driverless cars and trucks developed by entrepreneurs who had grown up on the nonprofit's properties traveling a test track at an industrial park the nonprofit would create in Westmoreland County from an enormous factory where Volkswagen once made cars and Sony once manufactured televisions.

The First Pittsburgh Renaissance

RIDC Is Born

Robert Pease came to Pittsburgh in 1946. Through a process unimaginable today, he arrived on the campus of the Carnegie Institute of Technology in the city's Oakland neighborhood, took an entrance exam, was accepted as a civil engineering student, and soon started classes. He had been raised in the American Midwest with its endless flatlands, farms, high sky, and clean air. Pease wasn't in Iowa anymore and the differences were stark. Southwestern Pennsylvania was a dense and dirty industrial region. Its largest rivers were working rivers. Their banks were lined with factories, expansive steel mills, coke works, and the rail yards and tracks that served them. Their waters were polluted with industrial and residential effluent. The region's voracious appetite for coal to heat homes and power industry darkened the skies with soot and tainted the air with noxious odors. "I woke up one fall morning in a barracks-style fraternity house and my upper lip was gray from breathing the air," Pease recalled of his first semester at Carnegie Tech. "It was really bad."

Postwar Pittsburgh had not shaken the reputation of being the grim place to live, work, and do business that had been its defining characteristic in the eyes of visitors for nearly a century. Many of those visitors pulled no punches when describing the conditions they found. "Six months residence here would justify suicide,"[1] said the 19th-century British philosopher Herbert Spencer. His biting review had to sting the Pittsburgh industrialist Andrew Carnegie, an admirer of Spencer, who had invited him to southwestern Pennsylvania to show off the steel empire he was building along the banks of the Monongahela River.

Nearly 50 years later, the story reported out of Pittsburgh was similar. "From whatever direction one approaches the once lovely conjunction of the Allegheny and the Monongahela [rivers] the devastation of progress is apparent," R. L. Duffas reported in *The Atlantic Monthly* in 1930. "Quiet valleys have been inundated with slag, defaced with refuse, marred by hideous buildings. Life for the majority of the population has been rendered unspeakably pinched and dingy."[2]

At the end of the Second World War, civic leaders despaired over what they feared would be a future of decline unless conditions improved. The poor quality of life not only threatened the health and well-being of the region's citizens, it was also a threat to the region's economic prospects. The local economy was already struggling to rebound from the Great Depression. Its major corporations were finding it difficult to recruit and retain quality professional talent, including executives.[3] Some corporate leaders were considering moving their headquarters out of smoky Pittsburgh to New York City.[4] Recruiting companies to move to Pittsburgh was equally challenging. Moreover, the economy was seen as vulnerable due to having an outsized share of its output and jobs invested in heavy manufacturing, particularly steel, whose future was increasingly a concern. The region lacked adequate infrastructure critical to growth, including modern highways and sanitary sewer systems. Downtown Pittsburgh, the region's center of commerce, suffered from low property values, neglect, congested streets, commercial blight, and a shortage of new development and investment. Pittsburgh's civic and business leadership, impatient with what little progress had been made to address the problems, decided bold steps were necessary.

To address those problems, a public-private partnership uniting government, business, and civic leaders was forged that over the following two decades would lead Pittsburgh from decline to renewal. The centerpiece of renewal was the first Pittsburgh Renaissance, an ambitious set of city-focused projects to reduce the insidious smoke, build new infrastructure, and redevelop downtown. It was led by a new nonprofit business consortium and the region's most powerful politician. In 1943, the nonprofit Allegheny Conference on Community Development was established to come up with a postwar agenda for improving the city and region and to rally community and private sector support. The Allegheny Conference counted 150 community leaders as members with an executive board that was dominated by the major corporations. But it was Richard King Mellon, the civic-minded Republican heir to the Mellon banking fortune, who most influenced the organization, and Mellon was committed to renewal. He found as a key partner in that endeavor David L. Lawrence, Pittsburgh's Democratic mayor, whose political influence reached from southwestern Pennsylvania to the state capital in Harrisburg, where he would later reside as Pennsylvania's 37th governor. New nonprofit authorities helped guide implementation of the agenda. They included the City of Pittsburgh's Urban Redevelopment Authority (URA), created in 1946 with the power to acquire land for redevelopment, and the Allegheny County Sanitary Authority, which would address the lack of sewage management and treatment that beset the city and surrounding municipalities. While many metropolitan areas throughout the United States were exhibiting symptoms of decline after the war, Pittsburgh became one of the first to move aggressively to reverse it.[5]

Clearing the air of the smoke that reduced the quality of life in the region and tarnished its reputation was a top priority. The City of Pittsburgh had passed a smoke control ordinance in 1941 during the administration of Mayor Cornelius Scully, who organized public hearings to muster support for it and blunt opposition, which included union coal miners. Smoky bituminous coal was the fuel of choice for home heating and industry. Finding a replacement was the key to reducing the heavy pollution. The ordinance required residents and businesses to switch from using bituminous coal for heat to a "smokeless fuel," such as a more expensive treated coal that burned more cleanly or natural gas. A report written by John P. Robin, secretary to the mayor, made it clear the city saw eliminating smoke as a key to its revival. Smoke control was technically possible, he wrote, and would "bring about a new era of growth, prosperity and wellbeing." The ordinance wasn't fully implemented until 1947, after Lawrence took office. A rapid transition to natural gas for heating began to relieve the city of its smoke problem. The ability to import large amounts of natural gas from the American

Southwest allowed for the wholesale change. The pipelines that made it possible had already been built by the federal government as a secure, interior oil transport route during the war, when German submarines hunting in Gulf Coast waters were sinking tankers and threatening oil shipments to Northeastern states. No longer needed for oil, they found new life transporting natural gas.

Pittsburgh converted to natural gas faster than any city in the nation. Three years after the city began enforcing its smoke control ordinance, only 32 percent of homes burned coal for heat compared with 81 percent a decade earlier.[6] The impact was dramatic. From 1946 to 1955 the number of hours of heavy smoke in the city had been reduced by 97 percent and hours of moderate smoke was reduced by nearly 89 percent, as recorded by the city's Bureau of Smoke Prevention.[7] Allegheny County followed with its own smoke control law in 1949. A majority of the region's largest manufacturers and steel mills resided in the county, outside City of Pittsburgh limits, and the county's smoke control ordinance was deferential toward those industries. The first set of county regulations, for example, only required coke ovens and open-hearth furnaces at steel mills to adopt pollution controls that were "proven to be economically practical." Neither ordinance addressed less visible air pollutants, such as fine particulate matter, which would remain a problem into the 21st century, particularly for the region's industrial river valleys.

But the dense smoke that had blanketed the region was all but gone. In the eyes of civic leaders, smoke control confirmed the possibilities they imagined for the city and region. "The change was so great. People noticed it," Pease recalled. He had witnessed the city's renewal under the Renaissance initiatives first-hand. He joined the URA during its early days as a young Carnegie Tech graduate, rose through the ranks to become its director, and later led the Allegheny Conference. "A lot of us have said, without any science behind it, that the people were so pleased with smoke control that Pittsburgh became a city that could do anything. I think some of the enthusiastic support for redevelopment that came later was a result of that can-do attitude."

The momentum of change brought much-needed improvements. Downtown Pittsburgh, the focus of several Renaissance projects, was given a facelift. Its historic "Point," where the Allegheny and Monongahela Rivers join to form the Ohio River, was cleared of the abandoned buildings, former exhibition hall-turned-city tow pound, warehouses, freight yards, saloons, and houses of prostitution that had made it a commercial slum. In their place, a new state park was built, offering welcomed green space for leisure and public access to the rivers that had long been denied. The URA undertook the first privately financed redevelopment project in the nation, building the modernist Gateway Center high-rise office complex adjacent to Point State Park. More parking garages were added. Once scarce, they had become a downtown necessity with the surge in suburban living and America's growing reliance on the automobile. Major highways, "parkways," were built connecting the city to the suburbs, Pennsylvania Turnpike, and Greater Pittsburgh Airport. The Port Authority Transit of Allegheny County was established in 1959, consolidating public transportation that until then had been operated by 33 private companies.[8] With a new plant, the Allegheny County Sanitary Authority began treating sewage from the city and more than 80 neighboring municipalities for the first time, improving the quality of water in the rivers. A series of federally funded dams and reservoirs was constructed to reduce the threat of flooding, one of the worst having been the St. Patrick's Day Flood of 1936, which swamped mills, neighborhoods, and the city's Downtown, claiming 62 lives and leaving 135,000 people homeless and thousands out of work.[9]

Meanwhile, concerns about the structure of the region's economy continued to weigh on civic leaders. The economic health of southwestern Pennsylvania relied heavily on the health of its manufacturing sector, particularly steel. Increasingly, studies warned that greater diversity was needed to avoid decline, including a 1946 report by renowned economist Charles Roos, a pioneer in mathematical economics, whom the Allegheny Conference and Chamber of Commerce brought in to look at the state of the regional economy.[10] More than 37 percent of the labor force in the southwestern Pennsylvania counties of Allegheny, Beaver, Butler, and Westmoreland were employed in manufacturing in 1950. Making steel and other durable goods accounted for more than

67 percent of those manufacturing jobs.[11] National comparisons under-scored the dominance of the region's postwar steel industry. The share of the local workforce employed in the primary metals industry was more than five times greater than the national average; in steel alone, it was nine times greater.[12] Moreover, thousands of jobs in the service, retail, and other sectors relied on supplying the mills and factories with what they needed, or on the paychecks their workers spent on food, housing, and consumer goods.

Wartime production had kept the steel mills busy. The United States Steel Corporation, the largest manufacturer in the region, emerged from the war profitable and with a larger workforce than before its outbreak. The American steel industry dominated the global market. It faced minimal foreign competition with war having destroyed steel mills in Germany and Japan and having badly damaged those in Great Britain.[13] But for how long? Foreign steelmakers were rebuilding, erecting modern mills, and developing new technologies while steelmakers in Pittsburgh continued production at costly integrated mills, many of which were built in the previous century and were becoming outdated. There were other concerns. The steel industry was highly cyclical, routinely experiencing spikes and slowdowns in demand that led to a cycle of layoffs and call-backs. The purchases they made and paychecks they cut tended to follow the pattern. Labor relations were tenuous. Crippling strikes loomed as a possibility whenever contracts neared expiration. Attracting and retain-ing companies that would diversify an industrial base so reliant on basic manufacturing was seen as critical to realizing a future of growth and prosperity. The region's economic imbalance was proof that diversity wasn't an organic process. But economists and civic leaders had reason to doubt whether southwestern Pennsylvania had the economic develop-ment capabilities to change the character of the local economy.

Revitalization's "Blind Spot"

In 1954, the Allegheny Conference and Pittsburgh Chamber of Commerce commissioned the Pennsylvania Economy League to look into whether the Pittsburgh metro region needed to do a better job at industrial development. Specifically, they wanted to know whether circumstances warranted creating a non-governmental, nonprofit organization dedicated to making the region more attractive to businesses and promoting a more diverse and stable mix of industries and jobs. The Economy League's report concluded the need for such an organization was "readily evident." Several findings supported that conclusion, but, generally, the researchers found that there was a lack of coordination among agencies involved in industrial development and that their effectiveness was uneven. Such shortcomings put the region at a disadvantage. Industrial development was becoming more competitive and complex, requiring a highly organized and coordinated approach, the study noted. And the stakes were high. "No region can expect to obtain a fair share of the anticipated future expansion in plant facilities and jobs or even to retain existing facilities and jobs without careful mobilization of its industrial development efforts to capitalize on its assets, adjust to its handicaps, and eliminate or mitigate its alterable deficiencies."[14] The recommendation of the study's authors was embraced by the Allegheny Conference, chamber, corporate leaders, and influential local politicians.

The first meeting of the Regional Industrial Development Corporation's board of directors was held in the late afternoon of August 8, 1955, in the board room of the Westinghouse Electric Corporation headquarters. The new organization had been established under Pennsylvania law a few months earlier as a nonprofit corporation "to coordinate, stimulate and provide . . . the selective industrial expansion and diversification of the Pittsburgh region by every reasonable means in order to maintain the economic stability of this region, provide expanded opportunities for employment and improve the standard of living of the citizens of the region."[15] Its charter had been approved by an Allegheny County Common Pleas Court judge before the board met. Civic leaders had preselected a board composed of leading business and civic leaders. The forces driving the Pittsburgh Renaissance were well represented. Pittsburgh mayor Lawrence was on the board and in attendance that afternoon. J. Stanley Purnell, secretary to Richard King Mellon, was the board's secretary-treasurer.

Clearly, the architects of the Pittsburgh Renaissance considered RIDC important enough to make sure they had a guiding hand in its governance. Purnell revealed the reason why. Economic development, he told *The Pittsburgh Press*, was the "blind spot" in the region's attempt to reimagine itself as a modern, thriving metropolitan region.[16] One of the board's first orders of business was to hire the organization's first president, who would shape its agenda and oversee day-to-day operations. They chose John Robin, the veteran political operative who had managed former Pittsburgh mayor Scully's campaign to win public support for the city's smoke control ordinance. Following the war, he had served as secretary to Mayor Lawrence and had been the first executive director of the city's URA. *The Pittsburgh Press*, when reporting his appointment, described him as Lawrence's "right hand man" and a Democratic Party "big wig" who had a reputation in Harrisburg and Washington, DC, as "the man who pushed through many of the deals that brought about Pittsburgh's renaissance."[17]

The RIDC board of directors and members of its operating committee read like a who's who of corporate Pittsburgh. Gwilym Price was elected chairman. Price, the chairman of the Westinghouse Electric Corporation, sent out dozens of invitations for seats on the board's operating committee.[18] While a few went to labor unions and educators, including the dean of Carnegie Tech's School of Industrial Administration, the majority of the committee's members would be men from the top ranks of powerful companies, such as U.S. Steel, Jones & Laughlin Steel, Equitable Gas, Duquesne Light, Mellon National Bank and Trust Company, People's First National Bank, the Baltimore and Ohio Railroad, and the regional branch of the Federal Reserve Bank.

The fact major companies with deep pockets were recruited as members was not a coincidence. For one, shortly after hiring Robin as president, the board approved a plan to raise money to cover RIDC's operating budget by soliciting annual contributions from companies as a condition of membership. Each would have a vote with the number of votes they controlled determined by the amount of money they contributed. The board made sure those votes couldn't be bought on the cheap, stipulating that "no contributions less than $1,000 per year [nearly $12,000 in 2024 dollars] would be accepted." The plan followed the logic of the Pennsylvania Economy League report, which suggested "the major regional business organizations, including the utilities and railroads, have the responsibility of providing both the operating and capital funds for the Corporation and thus should have the controlling voice in expenditure of these funds."[19] In its first year, RIDC raised more than $132,000—about $1.5 million in 2024 dollars—from member contributions, which accounted for nearly all of its revenue.[20]

With a budget, a small professional staff of four, and offices in Downtown Pittsburgh's Union Trust Building, Robin set out to meet the daunting challenge of expanding and diversifying the region's economy. Plentiful jobs and higher wages after years of depression, war, and rationing had fueled a nationwide boom in consumer spending and demand for housing, cars, appliances, and other products and services. Regions were positioning themselves to take advantage. Landing new and expanding companies was more competitive than ever. The Pennsylvania Economy League's report and recommendations offered RIDC a blueprint to follow.

One concept for redefining the industrial landscape that the Economy League was bullish about was the planned industrial district. The idea, which only a few U.S. metropolitan areas were exploring at the time, was to create communities of industries on subdivided tracts arranged in a park-like setting with utilities, streets, and other necessary infrastructure in place. Manufacturers were becoming less interested in building their own buildings, the Economy League noted. An attractive pitch would be to offer them a new facility as a package deal that included land, architecture and engineering services, construction supervision, and financing. "The community which is not equipped to provide such services quickly and on a package basis will rapidly lose its competitive position," the Economy League warned.

But it was unlikely that such industrial campuses would be created in southwestern Pennsylvania if left up to private developers, the report concluded. The market for planned industrial districts hadn't been established. Investing up front to prepare the site and build the infrastructure required a degree of faith, "which local realtors and other interests seem to be unable or unwilling to finance even though the opportunities appear to be sound."[21] RIDC didn't have the money to invest in planned industrial districts or a staff capable of building them. It was limited further by its charter, which didn't provide the latitude to acquire and develop land on its own. Robin felt RIDC should move in that direction, suggesting the organization should at some point consider establishing a capital investment program for "the purchase, development, and holding for good uses of industrial sites in the area."[22] The organization would pursue other strategies in the meantime.

A Research-Heavy Agenda

As a longtime political operative who took part in some of the most impactful deals of the Pittsburgh Renaissance, Robin understood the importance of forging personal relationships with influential people and made it a point of emphasis. RIDC "must develop, as far as possible, a personal relationship with the people, locally and nationally, who make industrial policy for major enterprises," he told the board at a May 1956 meeting at the Duquesne Club in Downtown Pittsburgh, where membership was exclusive to the city's wealthiest and most influential men. Several of those connections had already been made, and Robin was optimistic they would result in new industrial plants for the region.

Economic research would be another focus. Robin initiated a series of studies intended to provide a comprehensive understanding of the economy and the industries that contributed to it. The Economy League report had suggested RIDC conduct its own research rather than rely on "fuzzy academic studies" to build a base of knowledge that would inform strategies and actions. Topics for investigation included economic trends, production and consumption patterns, the industrial mix in the region, company needs, employment by industry, and an inventory of land available for industrial development and the condition of it. The research would "help segregate the myths from the facts of the area as a first step in eventually correcting both local and outside misconceptions about the area and . . . candidly placing the region's problems on the table." The report also suggested that RIDC study all major industries in the region and compile extensive data on everything from the supply of raw and semi-finished materials and concentration of production to labor skill requirements, their utility and transportation costs, and market patterns.

Research that would "segregate the myths from the facts of the area" could also be applied to solving another dilemma. Civic leaders fretted over Pittsburgh's poor reputation as a place to live and work. The Economy League complained that the dismal view of the region largely focused on its deficits—environmental and labor problems, for example—with little acknowledgment of its redeeming qualities, such as its store of technical research talent, labor skills, and cultural and recreational amenities, to say nothing of the sweeping improvements that were underway as renewal initiatives unfolded. They were dismayed by surveys that told them local business executives—"the one group who can do more than any other group or any amount of advertising or promotion to sell the Pittsburgh area to itself and to others"—were not only poorly informed about basic economic conditions in the region but were perpetuating its unflattering reputation beyond its borders. "I can't understand why anyone in business starting from scratch would want to locate in Pittsburgh or for that matter in Cleveland, Philadelphia, or any other highly industrialized area,"[23] said one executive of a "major Pittsburgh firm" who had been interviewed by Economy League researchers. Such comments were rarely supported by facts, they noted. In most cases, the region's strengths were never mentioned, and even when interviewers pointed them out, "they were glossed over."

More troubling were responses in surveys and interviews that suggested some executives who had soured on Pittsburgh were only keeping their companies in the region because of the investment that had already been made in their plants, which was seen as an indication of just how fragile the industrial foundation was. The Economy League concluded that a public relations strategy promoting a balanced view of the region's shortcomings and attributes was sorely needed. Robin felt RIDC was in position to do something about that. The young organization would explore a national public relations campaign, he said, to promote the region as an area suitable for industrial growth and a "center of purchasing power" that is in the midst of rapid urban renewal.[24]

But Robin would not stay around to see the project through, or any of the other initiatives he set in motion, for that matter. He resigned in 1957, less than 18 months after being hired as RIDC's first president, to take a job leading the Old Philadelphia Development Corporation, a public-private redevelopment agency that was revitalizing neighborhoods in the Center City district of downtown Philadelphia. Robin left proud of the work RIDC had accomplished so far, which was mostly limited to research. In his final board meeting, he pointed to an analysis of the economies of southwestern Pennsylvania and neighboring parts of West Virginia and Ohio, a study of labor relations and a report that looked at riverfront land suitable for industries that rely on water transportation. He hoped RIDC's work with a statewide bipartisan tax committee would result in lower taxes, especially on manufacturing, and create a more favorable climate for industrial development—an outcome that, he said, "might well be considered justification for the existence and support of [RIDC]" during his brief tenure.

CRISIS OF CONFIDENCE

How long RIDC would be able to justify its existence and support remained an open question. Despite months following promising leads, Robin admitted that little progress had been made in bringing new industries to the region. His successor, Edward Smuts, would encounter the same frustrations. Smuts, a veteran urban planner with the Pennsylvania Economy League and the City of Pittsburgh Planning Department, largely stayed the course set by Robin: a focus on economic research, industry assessments, building corporate relationships, and prospecting for sites to accommodate new or expanding companies. While the studies shed more light on the economic conditions of the region, stimulating industrial growth proved difficult. One obstacle was a shortage of available sites suitable for new or expanding companies. An RIDC inventory of "major unoccupied plants" in the region, for example, concluded that "there are very few good vacant buildings elsewhere in the region."[25]

The Pittsburgh Renaissance agenda was making impressive progress in other ways as the new decade approached. By 1959, the heavy soot that had obscured the skyline had dissipated. Dams and reservoirs were being built on the rivers to control flooding. In Downtown Pittsburgh, three modern high-rise office buildings rose in Gateway Center and a fourth was nearly finished. The commercial slum at the junction of the city's three rivers was being cleared for the new state park. Miles of the new Penn-Lincoln Highway connecting the city to eastern and western suburbs had been completed and more were under construction. But expanding and diversifying the economy remained the blind spot of renewal. Civic leaders, RIDC's board, and its members took note of the disappointing rate of progress. Contributions from members, RIDC's primary source of income, suffered and it was forced to obtain a bank loan that February to cover the gap in fundraising.

Board chairman Frank Denton, the chief executive officer of Mellon Bank, formed a committee to reevaluate RIDC's programs and budget. Smuts resigned as president in May 1959. He was replaced by Robert C. Downie, a former president of Peoples First National Bank, who would manage the reorganization. He oversaw the dismissal of RIDC's entire professional and clerical staff. Within a year, Downie was the only employee on the payroll.

The shake-up was accompanied by a directive from the board that RIDC would from there on out "place heavy emphasis on direct personal contacts and an aggressive sales program as the agency's principal effort in attracting new industry to the region." Denton explained that the decision to focus primarily on new industry and business prospects "underscores the fact that Pittsburgh has not capitalized on the improvement program to the extent possible by bringing in new industry and expanding job opportunities."[26]

For nearly 18 months, the board debated how RIDC could be refocused to spur industrial growth, or whether the organization had a future at all. RIDC found an advocate on the board in Pittsburgh mayor Joseph Barr. Barr, a former state senator representing Pittsburgh, was elected mayor in 1959 after Lawrence became the governor of Pennsylvania. During his 18-year career in the state Senate, Barr had helped pass legislation and secure state funding that was crucial to completing the city's Renaissance redevelopment agenda. He called a meeting of the board in September 1961. There, he argued that RIDC should be reorganized, restaffed, and its operations resumed. He backed it up with a pledge that the city would contribute $20,000 a year—roughly $244,000 in 2024 dollars—to the operating budget of the reformed organization. The board agreed. The search for a new president to lead RIDC began. For the first time, the board decided to look beyond southwestern Pennsylvania.

NEW LEADER, NEW VISION, NEW IDENTITY

The board found who they were looking for in Boston. They hired Robert H. Ryan, an accomplished commercial developer, as RIDC's third president in January 1962. The idea of creating planned industrial districts, or industrial parks, as a way to retain companies and attract new ones had been a consideration of RIDC leadership from the beginning. With Ryan, the board found someone who knew how to do it. He had been a vice president at Cabot, Cabot & Forbes, a Boston-area company that developed some of the first industrial parks in New England. The firm's 300-acre New England Industrial Center in Needham, Massachusetts, opened in 1948 as the largest master-planned industrial project in the country at the time. Its parks—which were characterized by a phased, market-responsive building program, preservation of the site's natural amenities, and consistent design standards—had become a prototype of early business parks worldwide.[27]

Three months into his presidency, Ryan set RIDC on a course that would come to define it. RIDC would become an operating development company. A new charter was approved that gave RIDC the authority to run such an operation. The board approved the basic tools RIDC needed in that role: a development fund to assist in financing development projects, and a real estate subsidiary for acquiring and controlling land and developing parks. Ryan began hiring development staff. He also established a scientific and research committee and gave seats to top local scientists, with the hope of capturing the commercial potential of ideas flowing from the region's universities.

By early summer 1962, only five months after he assumed office, Ryan was negotiating RIDC's first property deal. The opportunity to build its first industrial park awaited on a tract of lush farmland 10 miles northeast of the City of Pittsburgh that was being worked by gangs of prison inmates under the watch of armed guards on horseback.

The Workhouse
The Rise of Industrial Parks

The Allegheny County Workhouse and Inebriate Asylum first caught the eye of RIDC in a 1957 survey of potential sites for industrial expansion.[1] County officials had made it clear they would welcome the opportunity to get out of the business of running the prison, a stone fortress opened in 1869 along the Allegheny River in the Borough of Blawnox, about 12 miles east of the City of Pittsburgh. Its construction had been financed by selling interest-bearing bonds. For a time, its operating costs were covered by the sale of liquor licenses, a $1 million countywide tax, and profits from the labor of inmates.[2] But neither liquor license sales nor the special tax proved to be permanent revenue sources, and by the 1960s, unable to sustain the prison with the profits from inmate labor alone, the county was subsidizing it with general-fund tax dollars.

Inside, there were more than 1,000 cramped, narrow cells where upwards of 400,000 men and women had served their sentences over the prison's 102-year history. The inmates were a diverse group whose nationalities covered some 50 countries. The list of offenses that landed them in the workhouse was long. Although the workhouse had its share of inmates convicted of violent crimes, including murder and rape, most were there for minor offenses. Drunkenness, disorderly conduct, vagrancy, and being a "suspicious person" were among the most common. Others were incarcerated for offenses described in prison records as "keeping a bawdy house," "being a tramp," "being a nuisance," "being a scold," "incorrigibility," committing blasphemy, and "employing a lady waiter."[3] Not long after the dawn of the 20th century, the workhouse had earned the reputation as a place to punish socialists, striking workers, and others whose beliefs and activities irritated men with political influence at the time.

The inmates, mostly men, were put to work in shops within the workhouse walls making wooden barrels, brooms, brushes, carpets, chairs, and other products. Behind the prison and across Freeport Road—the main street in tiny Blawnox—stretched nearly 700 acres of county-owned farmland. There, inmates tended to cows, hogs, and other livestock. They worked the fields growing crops, including hay, alfalfa, corn, wheat, potatoes, beans, and peas. Apples were harvested from a fruit orchard. Flowers were grown in a greenhouse and sold to the public.

Despite the opportunity to work outdoors in fields, orchards, and fresh air, the conditions at the workhouse were generally considered harsh. Alexander Berkman, the most famous inmate to do time there, found conditions particularly difficult. Berkman, a Russian-born anarchist, had attempted to murder Henry Clay Frick, the partner of Pittsburgh industrialist Andrew Carnegie and chairman of the Carnegie Steel Company. Berkman was seeking retribution for Frick having sent 300 armed Pinkerton detectives to storm and retake the company's strike-bound Homestead steelworks in July of 1892. Seven union steelworkers were killed in the gun battle. Frick survived the assassination attempt. Berkman spent the next 14 years in prison, most of them in the state-owned Western Penitentiary on Pittsburgh's North Side, which he managed to tunnel out of only to be recaptured. The escape attempt bought him a transfer to the Allegheny County Workhouse to serve the rest of his sentence. "The ordeal of the day's routine is full of inexpressible anguish," he wrote in his memoirs. "Accustomed to prison conditions, I yet find existence in the workhouse a nightmare of cruelty, infinitely worse than the most inhumane aspects of the penitentiary. The guards are surly and brutal; the food foul and inadequate; punishment for the slightest offence instantaneous and ruthless. The cells are even smaller than in the penitentiary and contain neither chair nor table. Absolute silence prevails in the cell-house and shop. The slightest motion of the lips is punished with the blackjack or the dungeon, referred to with caustic satire as the 'White House.'"[4]

It was on the workhouse farm that Robert H. Ryan decided RIDC would build its first planned industrial district shortly after he became president of the nonprofit. The site was well suited for the park-like campus developed to high building standards that he believed would attract companies looking for light industrial, office, and research space, as had been the case with the industrial parks he had helped develop outside of Boston. The workhouse farm was pastural, undeveloped, and relatively close to the City of Pittsburgh. Its owner, Allegheny County, was eager to sell at a reasonable price. The planned extension of the Allegheny Valley Expressway, a limited-access highway, would cut along the southern edge of the farm, providing a quicker, more convenient route to Pittsburgh.

Negotiations with the county to buy the farmland began in the summer of 1962 with Ryan and Hiram Milton, whom he had hired as director of development, at the table. Milton was a rising star in the Democratic Party, the dominant political party in blue-collar southwestern Pennsylvania. He had gained economic development experience as a member or director of the Allegheny County airport, various planning committees, and a regional authority for municipal improvements. RIDC took on its new role as a real estate developer with a team that paired Ryan's experience as a developer of successful suburban industrial parks with Milton's political connections to the county and municipal officials who had influence over planning and zoning decisions and, in some cases, public funding. RIDC and the county reached a deal for the workhouse farm in March 1963, with RIDC agreeing to pay $1 million for 653 acres of county-owned workhouse farmland in what today is O'Hara Township.[5] The purchase was approved by the executive committee of the RIDC board at 11 a.m. November 22, 1963. They had little time to celebrate RIDC's new direction. One hour after they signed off on the deal, news broke that President John F. Kennedy had been assassinated in Dallas, Texas.

~

Ryan assigned a young, recently hired architect the task of getting the development of the new business park off the ground. Frank Brooks Robinson had been educated at Yale University and Carnegie Institute of Technology, which later became Carnegie Mellon University. In 1963, he was working at an architectural firm under the supervision of Dahlen Ritchey, a Pittsburgh architect whose work included such Downtown Pittsburgh landmarks as Mellon Square and the Civic Arena. Robinson came to RIDC by way of a chance conversation over lunch at the downtown Harvard Yale Princeton Club. "The club had a series of long tables, where you had lunch. You sat down next to whomever was there," Robinson recalled. "I didn't know the man next to me. He introduced himself, saying he was with the RIDC. I'd never heard of the RIDC." The man was Ryan, and Robinson apparently impressed him. "I went back to my drafting table. Dahl Ritchey came to me that afternoon and said that Bob Ryan wanted me to come and talk to him. He said to me that Ryan was probably going to ask me to join the RIDC and, if it didn't work out, I could always come back here."

Ryan was "a man of enormous energy" who was not without a few quirks, Robinson said. "He had a chip on his shoulder. He didn't like anybody of any wealth. He didn't like anybody of any authority. He had been invited here by the RIDC board, which was made up of senior people in the corporate world around here. He was going to show them what he could do. He had a wonderful secretary who was able to control his energy. When he would go off on these tirades about authority and that kind of stuff, she would calm him down." Ryan hired Robinson on the spot. "He said, 'I would like you, Robinson, to take on the development of this industrial park, the O'Hara [Township] park.' At that time, that was all I knew about it. But I knew that if I ran into trouble, I could always go back to the architectural firm."

Beneficial Deal, Inexpensive Money

The agreement negotiated with Allegheny County to buy the workhouse farm was well-suited to RIDC's financial circumstances at the time. Its new development fund couldn't afford $1 million investments and needed to grow. The county agreed to sell RIDC parcels of the farm piecemeal. The county would act as a land bank, selling parcels of at least 20 acres at a time when RIDC was ready to develop them. RIDC would install roads, water and sewer lines, and other infrastructure, arrange for the construction of buildings, and sell or lease the land and buildings on it to new or expanding companies. The proceeds from sales and leases, in turn, would bolster its development fund and the cash and equity it had on hand to invest in future projects. The ability to borrow large sums of money was critical to financing the projects. When it came to borrowing for construction at reasonable rates, RIDC had an advantage that private developers did not.

Legislation establishing the Pennsylvania Industrial Development Authority (PIDA) was adopted in 1956 to encourage and support job-creating industrial development projects. Its primary tool is a low-interest loan program that helps finance new business, research and industrial buildings, and parks that demonstrate to the satisfaction of the state their potential to create full-time jobs. Loans could be approved to cover up to 40 percent of a project's cost, sometimes more. The interest savings could be substantial, with PIDA loaning money at half the rate commercial lenders charge or lower. Eligibility for the low-interest loans during the early years of the program was limited. State law prohibited PIDA from loaning directly to private companies. Instead, the loans were made to nonprofits certified as regional industrial development organizations, such as RIDC. Those organizations would underwrite the loans, typically paying them off with money earned from the sale or leasing of the developed property.

Access to low-interest loans lowered building costs. Lower building costs enabled RIDC to offer companies more affordable facilities, whether through lease or sale. Such affordability only enhanced the package that RIDC offered to attract and retain companies and jobs, which included finding suitable sites, arranging financing and construction, and other services.

RIDC officials set out to recruit companies for the new industrial park. The approach was straightforward: get the word out to the contacts they made on the board and elsewhere, including those involved in research and development, burning a lot of shoe leather taking their pitch to business organizations, such as the Small Business Administration, the Lions, Kiwanis, and Rotary clubs, and making inroads with the region's universities. "You eat a lot of rubber chicken in the basement of a church and pretty soon people come to you and say, maybe you can help me with this," Robinson recalled. "They came to me when we talked about the PIDA program. For a business person, that's a wonderful incentive program and they could only get it through us."

The projects weren't limited to the workhouse farm property it was developing as an industrial park. In fact, the earliest were undertaken on land elsewhere that RIDC bought for the construction of free-standing buildings commissioned by a variety of companies and financed with PIDA and commercial loans. The first was a plant for the Globe Ticket Company, the nation's oldest ticket manufacturer, which had been looking to establish operations in Pittsburgh. Globe needed ready access to railroad lines, which ruled out sites on the workhouse farm property. Instead, RIDC found a parcel in nearby Blawnox against the rail line that ran along the banks of the Allegheny River. Other projects quickly followed, including buildings for a trucking firm in Etna Borough, Allegheny County, and a branch office for the American Institutes for Research, a nonprofit conducting behavioral and social science research.

~

Meanwhile, RIDC was working through the logistics of getting its first industrial park on the map. One unusual characteristic of the workhouse farm was that it was "no man's land," as Robinson put it. The land was owned by Allegheny County. It was not incorporated as part of the surrounding municipalities of Blawnox and Fox Chapel boroughs and O'Hara Township. One of the first orders of business was to convince one of those municipalities to adopt it and provide policing and other public services, including maintenance of roads and other infrastructure RIDC would install. In return, the park would generate jobs and the municipality would collect taxes on the developed properties. The search for a taker was more suspenseful than anticipated. Robinson first approached elected officials in Blawnox. "Blawnox said, 'Nuts to you, we're not interested.' They didn't believe [the industrial park] was going to happen. They thought I was out of my tree." Next was Fox Chapel, a wealthy bedroom community in the lush suburbs northeast of Pittsburgh. "I made no headway. I made my plea and they said we don't have industry in Fox Chapel." To his relief, O'Hara Township, the final option, agreed to incorporate the industrial park and provide the public services necessary for it to have a chance at becoming successful.

O'Hara Township was also willing to work with RIDC on its zoning requirements. RIDC envisioned building business, light industrial, and research spaces that were "different and better than what was offered elsewhere," Robinson said. The standards to which they would be built were drawn from Ryan's experience building similar parks in New England. The standards were specific down to the types of construction materials used. RIDC, for instance, eschewed the use of galvanized or other metal siding, which were among the most common materials used in southwestern Pennsylvania industrial building at the time. Instead, buildings in the O'Hara industrial park would be faced with brick. Protective standards were woven into O'Hara's zoning ordinance and written into the deeds of properties in the park. "Anybody who bought a piece of property got that with their deed and with that, they got us," Robinson said. "We were going to be the ones that say, first of all, whether you can build there and, second, what your building should look like."

Ten months after it agreed to buy the workhouse farm from the county, RIDC signed two companies to become the first tenants of the industrial park. The first was Clinical Products, a small medical supply company that was still in its early stages but had done well enough to consider expanding. It had outgrown its building and the owner was looking for a larger space when she heard Robinson's pitch for the RIDC O'Hara industrial park at a public meeting in Blawnox. "I would like to have a building up there, expand in your industrial park," she told Robinson. "That would be great," he replied.

Commercial lenders had shown little interest in giving the young company a sizable loan to finance a building. A low-interest PIDA loan would help make a new building easier on the company's budget. But even PIDA was hesitant about financing a building for a small company whose prospects for long-term success and employment were uncertain. RIDC and PIDA came up with a solution. PIDA would give RIDC a loan to help with the cost of the building, but RIDC would maintain ownership and lease it to Clinical Products. RIDC's ownership also assuaged the concerns of the banks, making commercial loans available. RIDC secured both, borrowing from Mellon Bank at an interest rate of 5.5 percent and from PIDA at 2 percent. Around the same time, RIDC put a second, more established tenant in the park, the Papercraft Corporation, selling 33 acres and a building it developed to the wrapping paper manufacturer founded by Pittsburgh entrepreneur Joseph Katz.[6]

O'Hara Takes Off

Development of RIDC O'Hara began in earnest, starting at Freeport Road and working back into the workhouse farm in phases, with RIDC buying more farmland from the county as interest in the business campus grew and new occupants were signed. The first phase, which covered about 150 acres, carried an estimated price tag in 1964 of $1 million, or more than $10 million in 2024 dollars.[7] Most would be financed through PIDA and commercial loans. Roads were built to Pennsylvania Department of Transportation specifications for carrying heavy trucks, which included concrete curbs and gutters. Sewers were laid. The park tapped into the spring-fed reservoirs that provided the workhouse with water and drew power from the lines serving the farm. The prison continued to operate the farm on the hundreds of acres of land that had not yet been purchased for the industrial park. For a time, contractors were installing infrastructure and constructing new buildings while inmates who tended nearby fields and livestock were flanked by armed prison guards on horseback to discourage any notion of attempting an escape.

With each new acre developed to RIDC's building standards and each new tenant signed, the O'Hara industrial park became more attractive to other businesses and further demonstrated the market for such campuses set in suburban greenfields, where none had been attempted before. Tenants ranged from a handful of start-ups and early-stage companies to some of the region's largest employers. Within two years, RIDC had developed buildings on the O'Hara campus for Westinghouse Electric Corp., which later expanded its footprint; Mellon Bank, the region's largest financial institution; and Thrift Drug, the dominant local drug store chain. More would follow, including technology companies, which RIDC's founders had sought to nurture as a key driver of a more diverse economy. Among them were Fisher Scientific, a Pittsburgh-based provider of instruments for the scientific research markets. Contraves Goerz, a defense contractor whose products at the time included lenses for submarine periscopes, would expand to occupy three buildings in the park, employing more than 1,000 workers at its peak.

As interest increased, the kind of buildings they could choose from broadened. In 1965, RIDC bought another 52 acres of workhouse land and introduced its first multiple-tenant building, a new concept at the park that offered smaller companies, particularly start-ups, 2,500-square-foot suites for lease that the designers called Townhouses for Industry. It was a speculative project with no tenants signed when the RIDC board approved the undertaking. Speculation that such a building would be a success was on target. The townhouses quickly gained popularity. RIDC would develop several others, including a series of "manors" at O'Hara, each named with a letter from the Greek alphabet. "We were seeing a number of professors from Carnegie Mellon University and the University of Pittsburgh starting their own companies," said Leon Gevaudan, who spent nearly 40 years working for RIDC as an engineer and former director of development. "They didn't have the resources to come in and build their own building. That was the idea of the townhouses. There would be incubator space. A company could locate there until it got through its first stages of development, then hopefully it would buy a larger piece of property in the park and build a facility specifically for their use."

One of the first start-ups to emerge from the universities and find a home at RIDC O'Hara was Extranuclear Laboratories, a scientific-instrument company later renamed ABB Extrel that was founded in 1964 by Wade L. Fite, a professor of physics at the University of Pittsburgh, who is considered one of Pittsburgh's first high-tech entrepreneurs.[8] RIDC put the start-up in its Alpha Manor multiple-occupancy building

but realized the company needed more than a building if it were to sur-
vive early stage challenges and pitfalls. Support services to help start-ups
reach stability and grow were lean in southwestern Pennsylvania, where
much of the applied research was done by major corporations with
resources in-house providing whatever was needed to move an idea from
the lab to the market. "Wade was a delightful person. But he was a phys-
icist, not a businessman," Robinson recalled. "He was pretty much at our
mercy. We didn't want him at our mercy. We wanted him to become
a business. So, we would introduce him to people who would help him
with the legal stuff, people who would help him with his marketing. He
was very responsive to that."

Not everyone was pleased with the progress at the O'Hara industrial park. Some private developers felt RIDC's access to low-interest
state loans that weren't available to them gave the nonprofit an unfair
competitive advantage and they would complain to local government
officials from time to time. PIDA loans were an advantage, to be sure.
Three years after RIDC decided to engage in commercial development,
it had completed 21 building projects financed in part with PIDA loans.
The companies occupying those buildings employed an estimated 4,000
workers.[9] Left unsaid was that at the time RIDC broke ground, private
developers weren't lining up to invest their time, energy, and money
in turning a suburban prison farm into the first industrial park in the
region. "You couldn't get a private developer to make an investment out
there," Robinson said. "They just wouldn't do it. There was no market.
There was too much risk. The industrial park was where we were taking
the risk to build spec buildings, to own them in order to have real estate
that would generate revenue for the operation of RIDC. If the private
developers didn't like that, at least they knew where we were."

Prospects turned even brighter in 1967. Expansion of the Allegheny
Valley Expressway—state Route 28—was underway. The highway ran
from the City of Pittsburgh eastward through the workhouse farmland
into north central Pennsylvania. RIDC sold 42 acres of the farmland to
the state for the new section of highway. It included an exit into RIDC
O'Hara, opening a high-speed transportation route to the industrial
park, which until then could only be reached by way of local roads slowed

by traffic, stop signs, and traffic lights. Ryan, buoyed by the new access to a highway, predicted the park would be "fully committed within one year after the completion of the expressway."[10] Development continued steadily, but Ryan's prediction proved overly optimistic, with the last parcel being sold for development in 2011.

∿

Ryan in only four years had shifted the identity of RIDC from a planning organization to a developer of commercial and industrial property with a public mission. Economic and market studies, once an RIDC staple, took a back seat to developing plants and buildings for companies as the means for expanding and diversifying the southwestern Pennsylvania economy. RIDC also shed a program to retrain displaced workers, which had been one of its original initiatives. About 75 percent of workers retrained had been placed in new jobs, which far exceeded expectations.[11] Such results suggested the program should be expanded. That was something Ryan believed was better suited for educational institutions, perhaps the community colleges that were emerging in the region. RIDC's finances were stronger than when he came on board. The development fund he established had committed more than $10 million to securing new homes for companies that in 1967 employed about 4,600 workers. The regional economy was strong and slowly becoming more balanced. But it was not enough to loosen the grip of steel and heavy manufacturing. "The region is far from the point where it could withstand a severe cyclical downturn in its primary metals industry," Ryan warned the board.

It was his last report to the RIDC board of directors. Ryan resigned as president in 1967 and left southwestern Pennsylvania to direct the development of Reston, Virginia,[12] as a planned city after Pittsburgh-based Gulf Oil Corporation took financial control of the project in the rapidly growing suburb of the nation's capital.[13] His resignation led to a reshuffling of RIDC leadership. It would be up to Hiram Milton, who succeeded Ryan as president, and Frank Brooks Robinson, who succeeded Milton as director of development, to guide an RIDC staff of fewer than 10 professional and clerical employees whose workload was rapidly becoming more demanding.

The regional population was stagnant at the beginning of the new decade. Yet, the workforce added more than 81,000 workers. It was a sign, Milton believed, that the regional economy was heading toward a stronger future in the next 10 years. And there was something noticeably different about the O'Hara industrial park. Gone were the inmates who once worked the undeveloped tracts at the Allegheny County Workhouse farm while contractors laid roads, sewers, and erected new buildings for businesses. The workhouse had fallen into poor condition. The state was assuming more of the incarceration responsibilities borne by counties. And it was clear the experiment of a self-sustaining prison had failed. In 1969, Stanley Hoss, a convicted rapist awaiting sentencing, escaped from the workhouse and went on a brutal crime spree, murdering a police officer he encountered in nearby Verona, Pennsylvania, and a young mother and her two-year-old daughter who he kidnapped in Maryland, before he was captured in Iowa.[14] The crimes and manhunt were national news. Allegheny County closed and razed the workhouse.

What undeveloped land remained of the workhouse farm was steadily being consumed by the industrial park. The first development phase of the park had been completed and fully occupied. The debt RIDC incurred to develop it had been repaid from the sales and leases it generated. A second development phase was nearly complete. Thirty-two buildings had been built, were in design or were under construction by the fall of 1971. Forty-three companies called the industrial park home.[15] RIDC, having demonstrated the market for an industrial park in the eastern suburbs of Pittsburgh, shifted its sights to the northern reaches of Allegheny County, where another large tract of unwanted government-owned land had become available.

Thorn Hill

The Thorn Hill School for Boys was a place that most boys growing up in southwestern Pennsylvania never experienced but may have heard about from a frustrated parent warning that it was where they'd end up if they didn't stop misbehaving. The reform school, opened in 1910, was a rural campus about 20 miles north of Downtown Pittsburgh in Allegheny County's Marshall Township and Cranberry Township in Butler County. It was cobbled together from eight farms—totaling nearly 1,500 acres—that the county bought for the purpose of housing, training, and educating delinquent boys aged 11 through 18 years who had been sentenced in juvenile court, most often for nonviolent offenses such as burglary, theft, truancy, and "incorrigibility."

As many as 500 boys at a time were housed at Thorn Hill, living in cottages supervised by "cottage parents." They spent half of their day in academic classrooms. They spent the other half working in the fields tending crops and livestock, their labor producing revenue that helped sustain the institution, much as the inmates had done at the Allegheny County Workhouse. In 1949, the sale of fruits, vegetables, and grains grown by the boys earned the school more than $1.2 million when converted to 2024 dollars, according to the superintendent's report.[16]

Thorn Hill's mission was to turn its young wards away from a life of offending to a life as law-abiding, productive citizens. School officials were impressed with their approach and the impact they felt it made on the lives of the boys. "The restless, undernourished, unstable boys who come to us are benefitted greatly by our active outdoors program of occupational activities, by the proper amount of sleep, bountiful meals and by the educational programs suited, as far as possible, to their abilities," they declared in a brochure.[17] The Pennsylvania Economy League, which studied the effectiveness of Thorn Hill for the county commissioners, found it to be a clean, orderly, and safe place where "the underlying attitude . . . appears to be one of helpful treatment rather than one of retributive punishment."[18] The report also noted, however, the school was too short-staffed to carry out a full youth development program that employed the highest standards known at the time. And it took issue with the value of the school's "active outdoors program of occupational activities," which were farm chores. "It is doubtful that on-the-job training in farm operations will be vocationally helpful to urban boys."

By the early 1960s, the human services approaches to delinquency were changing and the reform school land was seen as a valuable site for commercial development between the cities of Pittsburgh and Erie. The county got out of the reform school business, transferring 1,000 acres of the Thorn Hill school property to the state Department of Public Welfare in 1962. The state operated it as the Warrendale Youth Development Center before closing it 17 years later. The state and county were both interested in selling most, if not all, of the acreage they owned. RIDC was interested in buying it.

~

Several reasons argued against RIDC undertaking the development of a site significantly larger and more remote than the O'Hara industrial park. Development of the O'Hara park was ongoing and robust and RIDC was also arranging for the construction and financing of business, office, and research buildings and expansions elsewhere. Its small development division was stretched thin. By 1970, the division had dealt with 236 "company situations," which in addition to arranging financing and construction involved consulting, recruiting, site selection, and other services to attract companies to the region or keep them there.[19] Investing in a new industrial park at Thorn Hill was also not without risk. It was rural and remote. The main transportation artery was state Route 19, an aged two-lane backcountry highway. The market for an industrial park was purely speculative.

There was, however, a compelling reason to think Thorn Hill was worth the risk. A major four-lane highway was planned. Interstate 79 would start in West Virginia, travel north to Pittsburgh, and brush past the Thorn Hill property on its way to Erie, where motorists could connect to New York highways. Thorn Hill was also close to a Pennsylvania Turnpike exit, providing high-speed routes to states east and west.

The state agreed to sell RIDC 665 acres in 1970. RIDC would later buy nearly 300 more. Thorn Hill would be the largest development project RIDC had undertaken and the most challenging. The property straddled two municipalities and two counties. The municipalities were sparsely populated. Marshall Township, in Allegheny County, had only 2,907 residents in 1970;[20] Cranberry Township, in Butler County, had 4,873.[21] Electrical, phone, water, and sewage services were underdeveloped.

Zoning was a concern. Such issues would have to be worked out with local governments unfamiliar with large-scale development. "There was a lot of farm land," Gevaudan recalled. "I remember going to Cranberry Township for one of the first meetings with the municipality about the project. There was a stable underneath their meeting space. You could hear cows moving around."

Among the challenges of getting the Thorn Hill properties ready for development was the need to move a section of Brush Creek, which ran through the site. A more nettlesome issue was the lack of a sewage system in Marshall Township that could handle the demand of a large development. Federal grants helped the township build a major treatment plant. RIDC, which hoped the township would contribute to the cost of installing sewage lines, offered an incentive. Although it only needed lines 8 to 10 inches in diameter for the park, RIDC proposed laying oversized lines that could carry more than twice the capacity and having them extend into the heart of the township to accommodate future development. Marshall was poised for growth with the coming of Interstate 79 and township officials knew it. They accepted RIDC's offer and paid more than 60 percent of the cost of the sewage infrastructure.

RIDC followed the strategy that had worked well in O'Hara of developing the campus piecemeal, constructing buildings as companies were recruited to occupy them as a way to marshal its resources while establishing the market it hoped would attract others. The recession driven by the Organization of the Petroleum Exporting Countries oil embargo in 1973 didn't help matters.

Interest rates quickly increased. RIDC was still relying mostly on borrowed money to finance projects. The debt incurred developing the O'Hara park—about $8.5 million in 2024 dollars—was nearly paid off when RIDC began buying parcels at Thorn Hill. Milton told the board he was trying to "stretch dollars as far as possible" at the new industrial park to keep debt down.[22] RIDC received a grant from the federal Appalachian Regional Commission to help with site preparation costs, and its line on low-interest state industrial development loans led to considerable savings. In 1973, RIDC agreed to finance and build a research and development center for the national Society of Automotive

Engineers, the first organization recruited to Thorn Hill. Half of the project was financed with a commercial loan at 9 percent interest. Most of the remaining cost was covered by a PIDA loan with an interest rate of less than 1 percent.

Thorn Hill's distance from Downtown Pittsburgh—more than twice the distance from the city as RIDC O'Hara—was another recruiting obstacle. RIDC had built and sold buildings for two more companies and the U.S. Postal Service bought 80 acres on the Thorn Hill campus to open a bulk mail center, which was expected to employ 1,000 workers. But growth remained slower than hoped until construction of Interstate 79 was completed in 1976, Gevaudan recalled. "From that point, it really boomed." Five buildings were built for companies new to Thorn Hill within one year of the interstate's opening. Within two years, 14 buildings had been built, were under construction, or were in design, including the park's first multiple-tenant building.

MOMENTUM AND OPTIMISM

Just as Thorn Hill was gaining popularity, RIDC set its sights on establishing another industrial park, this time in the western suburbs of Pittsburgh, 15 minutes from Greater Pittsburgh International Airport. Westinghouse Electric Corporation owned the 355 acres located in North Fayette Township. It had designs of building its nuclear research center there but chose to locate it in the eastern Allegheny County municipality of Monroeville instead. Much of the land had been strip-mined, lessening its development value in the eyes of many. Robinson was less than thrilled about the railroad scrapyard on the property and mentioned that at an RIDC board meeting. Industrialist and investor Henry Hillman, whose Hillman Company was an RIDC member, responded, telling Robinson he'd buy the scrapyard land, clean it up, and build office buildings there. Hillman "saved the project," Robinson said. "I wasn't going to build anything with a scrapyard at the front door. Somebody had to come along with much deeper pockets than we had and get it out of there."

RIDC bought the Westinghouse land and began developing its third industrial park, Park West. Resting off of an interchange of a limited-access expressway, it offered a quick connection to both Downtown Pittsburgh and the airport. RIDC would later win federal foreign trade zone status for the site, an attractive feature for companies engaged in international commerce.

Within 15 years of having broken ground in O'Hara Township, RIDC had established itself as a central player in the economic development of southwestern Pennsylvania. It had proved adept at securing homes for new and expanding companies. It demonstrated the market for industrial parks at a former prison farm east of Pittsburgh, a reform school north of the city, and on abandoned, strip-mined land west of the city. By 1980, it had arranged the financing for and construction of more than 100 light industrial, office, and research buildings at those parks alone. More than half were on its O'Hara Township campus, where 77 companies were doing business. Sales, rent, and equity generated at the parks and reinvested in new projects had eclipsed revenue from membership fees as the nonprofit's chief source of income. RIDC was influencing economic development, policy, and the structural supports available

Frank Brooks Robinson was a seminal figure in RIDC's history, joining the organization's staff in 1963, serving in the administration of Governor Dick Thornburgh from 1979 to 1981, and returning to become RIDC's president—a position he held until 2003.

to sustain it. Its staff populated boards and commissions promoting economic growth and balance. RIDC leadership urged Allegheny County officials to do more to shepherd and finance development, going as far as lending the county staff to launch the Allegheny County Industrial Development Authority, which during its first five years would invest $334 million in projects that would create 12,000 new jobs.[23]

Southwestern Pennsylvania's economic landscape was slowly changing as a new decade approached. The health of the job market still greatly depended on the health of steelmakers and other manufacturers of durable goods, a characteristic that civic and business leaders still saw as the region's Achilles' heel. Several signs suggested a more balanced economy was not only possible, but on the horizon. Nonmanufacturing jobs were growing faster than manufacturing jobs. A U.S. Department of Commerce forecast for the region predicted the trend would likely continue.[24] But time was running out. A storm was gathering. The confluence of circumstances that leaders of Pittsburgh's postwar renaissance feared could happen was about to happen.

Steel Collapses and a Tech Center Rises

Just as RIDC's first business parks enjoyed steady growth in the 1970s, so too did the leafy suburban townships and boroughs they called home. More and more families migrated to suburbs with open space. Woods and farmland outside of Pittsburgh gave way to new housing developments, shopping centers, strip malls, and roads and highways to accommodate an increasing population of commuters. It was a different story in Pittsburgh's industrial suburbs.

Southwestern Pennsylvania's industrial corridors ran along its rivers, where massive steelworks and manufacturing plants lined the banks, several of them dating to the 19th century. The City of Pittsburgh had its share. The Jones & Laughlin Steel Company steelmaking complex, which reached from the city's Hazelwood neighborhood on one side of the Monongahela River to its South Side neighborhood on the other, was one of the largest in the region. The majority of the major steel mills and manufacturing plants, however, were located in boroughs and small cities outside of the City of Pittsburgh, including Clairton, Homestead, West Homestead, West Mifflin, Duquesne, McKeesport, Braddock, East Pittsburgh, Turtle Creek, and Donora in the Monongahela River valley; Aliquippa and Ambridge along the Ohio River; and Oakmont, New Kensington, and Brackenridge in the Allegheny River valley.

The mills and plants dominated the landscape, the economy, and the way of life in most of the industrial suburbs, none more so than those in the Monongahela River valley—known locally as the Mon Valley—the region's most heavily industrialized corridor. Taxes paid by the mills and plants were a chief source of municipal revenue on which public services depended, and in several cases steel companies provided some of those municipal services themselves. The wages of mill workers supported bustling downtowns with department stores, markets, libraries, restaurants, taverns, movie houses, and concert halls. Residential streets carved into the sides of the valleys were dense with houses, many of them of narrow, wood-framed construction that characterized the company housing of decades past. By 1980, the best days of the industrial suburbs were behind them.

Substantial gains in workers' wages and benefits helped fuel a steady residential migration away from the region's industrial suburbs, especially after World War II. As workers' purchasing power increased, the cars they bought widened the options of where they could live. Improved household finances improved their chances of getting a mortgage. Increasing numbers of them chose greener suburbs with space for a house and a yard over living against dingy industrial plants in towns choked with odorous smokestack emissions they once had tolerated as "the smell of money." The Borough of Duquesne, where U.S. Steel operated its Duquesne works, lost more than half of its population between 1930 and 1980. On the other side of the Monongahela River in McKeesport, home of the U.S. Steel National Tube works, 44 percent of the city's residents left between 1940 and 1980. Meanwhile, the southwestern Pennsylvania population as a whole remained relatively stable, indicating that most of those who left the mill towns did not flee the region, but relocated within it. The beneficiaries included O'Hara Township, where RIDC built its first industrial park. Its population doubled between 1940 and 1980.[1]

What happened next would not only hasten the decline of the once-prosperous industrial suburbs, but would reverberate throughout southwestern Pennsylvania, leading to a historic exodus of jobs, people, and investment the magnitude of which few U.S. metropolitan regions have experienced.

∼

The fall of steel and heavy manufacturing in southwestern Pennsylvania did not come without warning. Postwar studies had argued for the diversification of the region's economy as a hedge against a contraction of the primary metals industry that researchers warned was likely. The most comprehensive of the studies was commissioned by the Pittsburgh Regional Planning Agency, a predecessor of the Southwestern Pennsylvania Commission. Released in 1964, it found the competitiveness of the region's steel industry had steadily eroded and predicted steep losses in primary metals jobs by 1985.[2] Such concerns had been shared by the leaders of the first Pittsburgh Renaissance, who had established RIDC to stimulate job growth and rebalance the economy with a more diverse mix of employers as part of their urban renewal agenda. Greater urgency and resources, however, were directed toward revitalizing Downtown Pittsburgh, the central focus of their agenda.

Integrated steelworks, several of which were built nearly a century earlier, characterized the industry in southwestern Pennsylvania. Each housed all of the furnaces, mills, and shops necessary to turn iron ore into finished steel products: blast furnaces that drew iron from ore, open-hearth furnaces and Bessemer converters that purified iron into steel, shops that serviced and maintained the steelworks, and a network of mills that turned unfinished steel into rail, beams, wire, plates, and other products customers demanded. Integrated mills were huge. Each employed thousands of unionized workers, some as many as 10,000 or more. The U.S. Steel Homestead Works covered 430 acres. Such plants faced daunting challenges after World War II. Labor costs were escalating. The drive to innovate, which had fueled their rise to power, had steadily waned. Companies were slow to adopt new technologies and reluctant to reinvest in aging facilities that were becoming less competitive. They faced stiff competition from foreign steelmakers who operated modern, more efficient plants. Domestic "mini-mills" were capturing more of the market making steel from scrap in electric arc furnaces— a less capital-and-labor intensive process, against which southwestern Pennsylvania's older, integrated steelworks struggled to compete.

The industry's weaknesses were not outwardly apparent when Pittsburgh baseball fans celebrated the Pirates' World Series victory over the Baltimore Orioles in the fall of 1971. Steel production had soared in 1969, driven by the military build-up during the height of the Vietnam War. Pittsburgh's unemployment rate fell to 2.1 percent in October of that year, which was not only well below the national average, but lower than the lowest rates reported during the robust 1950s.[3] Only six years earlier at its Duquesne works, U.S. Steel started up its Dorothy Six basic oxygen process blast furnace. The world's largest blast furnace at the time, it was the company's most technologically advanced, although the basic oxygen process had been adopted more than a decade earlier in Europe and the Soviet Union. As a major capital investment in modernization by a company slow to adapt to changes in the industry, it read as a welcome signal the region's largest steelmaker had confidence in the future.

The downsizing of the American steel industry intensified soon afterward. Companies started closing mills with regularity across the country. Between 1974 and 1979, U.S. Steel alone closed more than 40 plants. Still, it was not clear in Pittsburgh that the dominoes were about to fall. None of the company's major operations in southwestern Pennsylvania were among those shuttered, with the closures mostly limited to the company's smaller facilities across the country. But a U.S. Steel press conference on September 27, 1979, left steelworkers, public officials, and anyone with a stake in the steel industry with the sinking feeling that the worst was yet to come.

THE BOTTOM DROPS OUT

Speaking at the company's Grant Street headquarters in Downtown Pittsburgh, U.S. Steel chairman David M. Roderick announced sweeping cutbacks. Fifteen more of the company's plants and mills in eight states were being closed, including some of its major operations. More than 13,000 workers would lose their jobs. The closures hit close to home: two plants would be closed within the sprawling Homestead Works, once the mightiest steelworks in the world. The rest of the Homestead Works were to remain open, for now. Youngstown, Ohio, was not so lucky. The company's Ohio Works 65 miles northwest of Pittsburgh was on the list to be closed, eliminating 3,500 jobs. A day after the U.S. Steel announcement, Jones & Laughlin Steel revealed it would close its Brier Hill works in Youngstown. Two years earlier, Youngstown Sheet and Tube had started the process of shuttering its steelworks, which had employed 4,000 workers.[4]

The steel industry had always traveled a bumpy road of labor strikes, cyclical swings in demand, and layoffs, only to have jobs and productivity return. This was different. Major plants were being shuttered, many soon to be razed. Pittsburgh had already watched the Heppenstall Steel Company close its works in the city's Lawrenceville neighborhood one year earlier. Jobs were being eliminated, not temporarily suspended.

Roderick was determined to return U.S. Steel to profitability. The company expected to post a large fourth quarter loss in 1979. Its older integrated mills were among the biggest money-losing operations, which was ominous news for southwestern Pennsylvania. He warned the company would consider further actions "to accomplish our long-range objective of making steel operations an attractive business investment."[5] Layoffs became more frequent, even at plants not on the list to be closed, as the company moved to cut its losses.

The repercussions on the region's economy were not immediate. RIDC closely followed the data, assessing the economy's strengths, weaknesses, and where it might be heading. Hiram Milton, its president, conveyed a sense of relief in November 1980 when he told the board the local economy had "displayed surprising strength," reporting that although recent layoffs in the steel industry hurt, total employment in the region had risen slightly over the past 12 months.[6]

One positive sign was that RIDC's development division remained busy. The nonprofit had recently arranged the financing for a major expansion of the Giant Eagle supermarket chain on 62 acres in the City of Pittsburgh. Eight buildings had been completed during 1979 at the O'Hara and Thorn Hill industrial parks, and 15 others were under construction. Those projects alone accounted for 1,100 jobs.[7] RIDC was seeing an increasing number of technology companies expand. All of Beta Manor II and an adjacent building at the O'Hara park were occupied by two research divisions of Westinghouse, which built a bridge between the two. The tech company Contraves Goertz, which employed 600 people at O'Hara, added another building to make space for another 165. With RIDC's help, PPG Industries undertook a major expansion of its Coatings and Resin Research Development Center in suburban Hampton Township east of Pittsburgh.[8]

"Greater diversity in the economy is evident," Milton declared in his report to the board on November 19, 1981. The regional economy has "held up reasonably well considering the slack in the national economy and steel layoffs," he added, reporting that employment had expanded by more than 48,000 jobs over the year, despite the downturn in manufacturing.

It would be Milton's final report as president. He resigned in 1981 to lead an initiative organized by the Allegheny Conference on Community Development to set long-term regional economic development goals and determine how to accomplish them. RIDC, which joined the initiative, agreed to continue to pay his salary, in effect loaning Milton to the new endeavor. Frank Brooks Robinson was named Milton's successor. He had recently returned from Harrisburg, where he served in the administration of Governor Dick Thornburgh as executive deputy secretary, acting secretary of the Pennsylvania Department of Commerce, and executive director of the cabinet's economic development committee. He previously had spent 15 years with RIDC having risen to vice president and director of development.

RIDC had experienced significant financial growth since its early days when it relied almost exclusively on the contributions of its members to stay in operation. When Robinson took office, finances were healthy enough for the board to discontinue member contributions, which had come to account for a smaller share of the nonprofit's revenues as income from the sale and leasing of buildings increased. Its ambitious list of development projects could continue as long as it had access to loans to help with the financing of them, particularly low-interest PIDA loans. RIDC's total assets had increased. In 1981, Milton reported the nonprofit's fund balance had increased by $1.4 million, which reflected income over expenses. Although RIDC owed $12 million in mortgages and notes and another $11 million in PIDA mortgage liabilities—a debt-to-net-worth ratio the board felt was "rather heavy"[9]—the sources it relied on to pay down the debt seemed secure as companies continued to buy and lease its buildings.

Robinson assumed office as the United States entered into recession for the second time in less than 10 years. One year later, economic data began to reveal staggering job losses in the region as turmoil in the steel industry spread.

~

The flicker of hope that the southwestern Pennsylvania economy might avoid catastrophe expressed in Milton's final report to the RIDC board was extinguished in Robinson's first, which he delivered on November 24, 1982. He characterized the regional economy as "bleak," noting that unemployment had risen from an already troubling 12.5 percent to 14 percent over the previous three months. "The impact from steel layoffs and shutdowns has been dramatic, and there has been a loss of momentum in industrial growth and diversification. The economic situation has placed a tremendous strain on local communities and a greater burden on survivors for the providing of essential services."[10]

Southwestern Pennsylvania was not alone. America's dominance in the steel industry had slipped away. Steel made in the United States had accounted for nearly 60 percent of the steel produced in the world in 1920. By 1984, American steelmakers were producing less than 12 percent of the world's output, a smaller share than their competitors in Europe and Japan.[11] The consequences were broadly felt across America's industrial heartland. The Pittsburgh region, lacking modern plants, was among the most vulnerable. Once the center of U.S. steelmaking, it had lost its competitive edge. The fallout would be devastating.

Destruction of the southwestern Pennsylvania steel industry came swiftly. Mill closings and the consequences became routine stories in the newspapers and on the evening news as one after another was closed, often in piecemeal fashion over months and years—shop by shop, furnace by furnace, mill by mill.

In 1983, U.S. Steel announced it would close two of its major southwestern Pennsylvania steelworks. One was the Duquesne works in the Mon Valley, which once employed as many as 9,000 workers. Included was the Dorothy Six furnace, which the company had christened 20 years earlier as the most technologically advanced in its vast inventory of furnaces. The company also announced the closing of its American Bridge works in Ambridge, a city named after it in Beaver County. It had employed as many as 4,500 steelworkers, who made steel for structures ranging from the mundane to the extraordinary, including the Empire State Building, the Houston Astrodome, and the gates of the Panama Canal.[12] The following year, LTV Steel closed its Aliquippa works, also in Beaver County, eliminating 8,000 jobs at the plant, which as a major defense contractor during World War II made steel for ship hulls and tank armor. In 1985, ARMCO closed its tubular steel plant in Ambridge, dealing another blow to the small Beaver County city. The dismantling of the former Jones & Laughlin Steel Company's steelworks in Pittsburgh begun years earlier was nearly complete. The steelworks, which had been purchased by LTV, had employed as many as 12,000 workers.

Then, on a hot July day in 1986, U.S. Steel's Homestead Works, the most famous steel plant in the world, closed its doors. The steelworks had a footprint in four municipalities, employed 15,000 workers—as many as 20,000 during World War II[13]—and produced more than 200 million tons of steel in its 105-year history. Its rails fueled the nation's westward expansion. Iconic skyscrapers and bridges were built from the beams it produced. Its plates modernized the U.S. Navy. When Soviet Union premier Nikita Khrushchev toured the United States in 1959, he had the Homestead Works on his short list of places to visit—along with Hollywood and a farm in the Midwest—only to find the steelworks closed by a national steelworkers' strike when he arrived.[14]

Wheeling-Pittsburgh Steel also closed most of its Monessen Works in Westmoreland County in 1986, where as many as 3,500 steelworkers had been employed. In 1987, U.S. Steel closed its National Tube Works in the Mon Valley city of McKeesport, which had some 6,300 workers on its payroll in the 1960s. The same year, LTV Steel closed most of its Ambridge Works, dealing the industrial county yet another setback. More closings would follow, including steel industry suppliers. Among the casualties was the Mesta Machine Company, a manufacturer of steel-making machinery that employed more than 3,800 workers and had operated next door to the U.S. Steel Homestead Works since 1898.

The assets of the company, whose machinery could be found in some 500 steel mills, were sold in 1983 not long after it had filed for bankruptcy under the threat of foreclosure.

Unemployment soared. The number of jobless southwestern Pennsylvania workers more than doubled between August 1981 and January 1983, rising from 88,500 to 212,400. The rate of unemployment reached 18.2 percent regionwide, much higher than the national average of 10.5 percent and rivaled only by the darkest days of the Great Depression, when the nation's jobless rate peaked at 25 percent of the U.S. workforce. In Beaver County, unemployment surpassed Great Depression highs. Peaking at a staggering 28 percent in March 1983, the jobless rate in the beleaguered county would remain above 15 percent for another 20 consecutive months. Most of the regional job loss was the result of plant closures. Most of the losses were permanent. Most were concentrated in manufacturing, driven by heavy losses in the primary metals industry.[15]

Southwestern Pennsylvania's powerful manufacturing sector, built over the course of more than a century, would be dismantled over two decades. Manufacturing had accounted for nearly one-third of jobs in the region in 1970, a significantly higher share of overall employment than was found in the nation as a whole. By 1990, manufacturing's share of the region's employment had dwindled to about 14 percent, much lower than the national average.[16] In all, the region would lose more than 142,000 manufacturing jobs from 1978 to 1998, with all but 11,000 of them eliminated in industries that produced durable goods, mainly primary metals.[17]

STARING INTO THE ABYSS

The economic shock was still fresh in 1983 when Robinson reported to the RIDC board in May. While the national and state unemployment rates had begun to decline, the local jobless rate continued to rise. Southwestern Pennsylvania "has not yet experienced the beginnings of a recovery" and the "situation remains quite fragile," he told them. Yet, he managed to strike a note of optimism. The region, he said, "still exhibits some underlying strengths which may offer some exciting opportunities."[18]

Among the opportunities he saw was enlarging the region's portfolio of high technology companies, whose potential for growth was increasingly seen as an economic catalyst. Another was the expansion of RIDC facilities leased to small businesses, which had helped to inject some welcomed balance in the economy before the collapse of steel. A third opportunity was to spread RIDC's expertise in developing industrial parks to counties outside of Allegheny, where the nonprofit had concentrated most of its development up until then.

But there were headwinds. While there continued to be interest in RIDC's industrial parks, much of it was in the form of inquiries rather than commitments, which had fallen off. Construction of new buildings and expansions had slowed. Borrowing was more expensive. Commercial loan rates were as high as 16 percent. Low-interest state development loans became more expensive with changes to the PIDA loan program. Interest on PIDA loans, which at times had been as low as 1 percent, jumped to 7 percent. A $500,000 loan limit was imposed, raising concerns that the lower ceiling would discourage major projects, such as buildings for large firms looking to expand.[19] Another issue was the diminishing image of the region and Pennsylvania as places to do business. A recent national survey, which attempted to measure the desirability of states in terms of industrial development, ranked Pennsylvania 44th out of the 48 continental U.S. states. "The stigma of such reports clouds our marketing efforts, not unlike that of the 'dirty Pittsburgh' stigma that we labored with for so long," Robinson complained.

RIDC could still lean on the rental income it was earning from the buildings it leased to companies, mostly in its industrial parks. Rental income, which was its chief source of revenue, had increased slightly to reach $2.3 million in 1982. The nonprofit also continued to find companies willing and able to buy its buildings, selling six each at its O'Hara and Thorn Hill parks that year. The foreign trade zone at Park West was open and operating at a profit. And RIDC could cull regional industrial assistance programs to supplement financing packages for companies looking to grow and hire, including support for small and minority-owned businesses and money for infrastructure improvements, machinery, equipment, and working capital.

While RIDC's focus remained fixed on financing and developing buildings to attract and retain companies and jobs, its involvement in resuscitating the southwestern Pennsylvania economy was expanding in other directions. It conducted extensive interviews with high-tech companies and research universities to understand what needed to be done to unlock their potential as economic engines. The relationships formed with the universities, in particular, would quickly develop into fruitful partnerships. RIDC worked with Penn's Southwest, a nonprofit that marketed the region to new companies, to establish the Pittsburgh High Technology Council, one of the first local organizations to nurture advanced technology as a rising sector of the economy. RIDC served as an unpaid consultant to the Allegheny County Industrial Development Authority, which was investing hundreds of millions of dollars to make companies more competitive and create jobs. It worked with the Allegheny Conference on Community Development to create a job bank to match displaced workers with new employment opportunities. When a business-led organization in McKeesport was formed to plot the revitalization of the Mon Valley, RIDC joined as a consultant to study the economic conditions and prepare a plan for action, loaning one of its 11 employees to work on the initiative full time.[20]

Such activities reflected the urgency that swept through the region. Government, civic and business leaders, university presidents, researchers, and others responded with surveys, studies, committees, and task forces as they rushed to understand what had happened and what the options were, and to agree on a strategy to point the region toward a new economy. Meanwhile, fear, frustration, and anger spilled out of the Mon Valley.

⌒

The closing of the mills was painful. Household incomes disappeared for steelworker families in mill towns and in the suburbs where many of them had moved. The regional and national economies had been weakened by a brutal series of recessions begun years earlier. Displaced steelworkers found few job opportunities outside the plant gates. Jobs that paid as much as they had earned in the mill were even more scarce. Disbelief gave way to confusion and uncertainty. Another round of layoffs and word that another steelworks would close or partially close dampened the faint hope the industry would rebound, that the mills whose steel had been essential to the building of modern America would be saved.

Groups mostly consisting of union workers and community activists formed to advocate for aid for the increasing number of unemployed and for reinvestment in the region's industrial suburbs. Aside from organizing rallies and marches, their tactics tended to differ. The Tri-State Conference on Steel, for example, unsuccessfully attempted to convince municipal officials in towns where mills were closing to take possession of them through eminent domain and restore them to competitiveness with money raised through the sale of bonds. The Denominational Ministries Strategy, a group of Protestant clergy and union members, used more confrontational, attention-grabbing tactics to keep the spotlight on the worsening conditions in the steel valleys. Its activities ranged from organizing workers to withdraw their savings from Mellon Bank to having its members rent safe-deposit boxes and secretly stuff them with dead fish, causing the banks to reek of spoiling fish a few days later.

U.S. Steel, which owned many of the mills that were closing or downsizing, was a natural target of protest, particularly after announcing its purchase of Marathon Oil for $6.4 billion (about $21 billion in 2024 dollars) in December 1981. The company also would change its 85-year-old name to USX, restructure, and reduce its steelmaking operation—once its primary business—to one of four operating units. The Marathon announcement had stunned and angered workers, their unions, and municipal officials in struggling industrial suburbs, who argued the company should have spent the money on modernizing its outdated steelworks to make them competitive again. U.S. Steel chairman Roderick responded that while the company was able to raise the huge sum it needed to buy Marathon Oil, it could not obtain money to upgrade its steelworks.[21] Protestors saw local banks as reluctant to invest in crumbling steel towns. Protests against Mellon Bank intensified after it and two other banks foreclosed on steel-mill equipment manufacturer Mesta Machine. Mesta filed for bankruptcy, which froze its bank accounts—including wages owed employees—and led to its quick demise.

The unrest also found RIDC. An attempt was made to occupy its Downtown Pittsburgh offices in 1983 by local members of the Association of Community Organizations for Reform Now (ACORN), who were protesting the grim circumstances of the unemployed. The confrontation was brief and ended without incident. But it caught Robinson off guard. RIDC was working to keep jobs in the region and create new ones. It was working with others to establish a job bank for the unemployed and help a steel town find a path to recovery. "The ACORN invasion angered me," Robinson recalled. "They were after the wrong target, in my judgment. We were trying to do what they were after. Everybody was all mixed up at that time. And they were angry."

Several of the protestors' targets figured prominently on the RIDC board of directors, however. U.S. Steel was represented by two of its executives in 1983, including Roderick. LTV Steel's chairman was on the board. So were executives of three of the largest banks in the region, including Mellon Bank chairman J. David Barnes, who was on the board's executive committee. Also on the board were executives of utilities and other major companies, the presidents of the University of Pittsburgh and Carnegie Mellon University, executives of economic development organizations, the executive director of the Urban League, the president of the Allegheny County Labor Council, the mayor of Pittsburgh, and county commissioners from Allegheny, Beaver, and Butler counties.[22]

RIDC, its mission, and methods were poorly understood in the region. It did not employ a public relations specialist. It did not schedule press conferences or seek news media attention in other ways to publicize its accomplishments. To most of the populace, RIDC was little more than an acronym on a sign marking the highway exit to one of its industrial parks. The low public profile was intentional, Robinson said. His reasoning: "The whale that spouts gets speared." Keeping a low profile would become more difficult as RIDC began to aggressively address the decline of the industrial suburbs as a developer.

THE FIRST BROWNFIELD

The Jones & Laughlin steelworks in the City of Pittsburgh was among the first major steel operations to fall. Its fiery mills and furnaces covered two city neighborhoods on opposite sides of the Monongahela River. The first to be built was its Pittsburgh Works on the northern banks of the river in the city neighborhood of South Oakland on land the company purchased in 1859, where it erected two blast furnaces it named Eliza. The Pittsburgh Works would come to boast four additional blast furnaces, coke ovens, and strip, bar, and other mills. A "hot metal bridge" spanned the Monongahela connecting the two J&L works, enabling ladles of molten iron to be hauled from the Eliza furnaces to the South Side Works by rail. There, open hearth furnaces and a Bessemer converter removed the remaining impurities from the iron, turning it into steel. The Pittsburgh Works was particularly productive during World War II, receiving the U.S. Army-Navy "E" Award for excellence after making enough steel to build 32 armor-plated ships during a single month in 1943. Not to be outdone, its No. 18 bar mill set a world production record, making more than 44,000 tons of bar during a single month in 1944.[23]

In 1968, J&L sold controlling interest in the company to Ling-Temco-Vought, Inc., which became LTV Steel. A decade later, as the decline of steel intensified, the new owners were interested in selling the largest steelmaking complex in the city. In 1981, the Charleston, West Virginia–based Park Corporation bought a shuttered hot strip mill on 48 acres at the Pittsburgh Works, about three miles upstream from where the Monongahela joins the Allegheny to form the Ohio River. The company had been acquiring old, troubled industrial sites for redevelopment or for the value of their machinery and other assets. For RIDC, the Urban Redevelopment Authority of Pittsburgh, and others, the value of the site was its proximity to the city's research universities two miles away.

Robinson, in his first year as RIDC's president, was concerned the Park Corporation's intention was not to redevelop the mill site for industrial tenants, but to "raze it, take everything of value from the property and then dump it." RIDC and the URA envisioned a place along the river that could attract university researchers and advanced technology companies as an extension of the innovation corridor through the city's Oakland neighborhood. Park took the equipment that remained and sold the site to the URA in 1983. The mill structures were razed and sold as scrap.

RIDC agreed to work with the URA as an advisor and chief developer of the Pittsburgh Technology Center,[24] conceived as an urban research park nestled in a campus-like setting with a riverwalk, tree-lined sidewalks, and other aesthetic features. Private developers would be sought to develop parcels at the site as well. The University of Pittsburgh and Carnegie Mellon were recruited to participate in the planning with the idea their researchers, labs, and institutes would occupy some of the buildings with private technology companies occupying others. The strip of riverfront would be retained by the city for restoration, although turning industrialized riverfronts into city attractions would not gain momentum for another decade. The state of Pennsylvania invested heavily in the vision. By 1988, it had contributed nearly $17 million toward development of the Pittsburgh Technology Center, $14 million toward a building for the University of Pittsburgh, and $17 million toward a building for Carnegie Mellon.[25] The financial risk to RIDC was limited. It agreed to make a $1.3 million "rolling contribution," which could be called upon to keep the project moving while the URA awaited receipt of state funds. RIDC's money could be tied up for 10 years, but it would be repaid as development progressed with the advances leveraged against land purchases.[26]

Civic leaders and government officials greeted the plan to redevelop a discarded steelworks as a center of technology innovation with unbridled optimism. University of Pittsburgh president Wesley Posvar saw the Pittsburgh Technology Center raising Pittsburgh's image as "biotech valley" and becoming an "incubator for an exciting new industry that will . . . infuse new economic vitality into the area." Carnegie Mellon University president Richard Cyert foresaw a "beautiful place that becomes a statement of the new Pittsburgh." The URA believed it would "secure Pittsburgh's place as a leader in the technology sector while symbolizing the dynamic transformation of the city's economy" into one

Workers at the Duquesne (top left and bottom left) and McKeesport (above) plants. Credit: Rivers of Steel

diversified by its strengths in research, new product development, and advanced technology. Pittsburgh mayor Richard Caliguiri pronounced it the "most important economic development project undertaken in Pittsburgh in the past 40 years."[27]

For all of the enthusiasm, the Pittsburgh Technology Center was slow to develop. There were upwards of a half dozen participants with a stake in the outcome, far more than RIDC had worked with on previous projects. Planning by the city and sorting out the funding took time. It was the first time RIDC attempted to redevelop a large, vacated industrial plant. The URA had never done so, either. Brownfield redevelopment was only beginning to be attempted elsewhere in America. There were lessons to be learned. The demolition, remediation, and redevelopment of industrial sites was a long and expensive journey rife with uncertainties. It would be 10 years before the first building at the Pittsburgh Technology Center opened.

Environmental inspections found tar pits, waste oil, more than 400,000 gallons of oily water, and ferrous cyanide. The tar and water were discovered and dealt with first. The ferrous cyanide, which was found later during construction, delayed progress and gave prospective private developers reason to exercise caution before investing. Never completely knowing what surprises lie beneath old industrial plants sites proved to be an enduring characteristic of brownfield development. The source of the cyanide, it turned out, was not the J&L strip mill, but a waste pit in a mid-19th-century coal gasification plant that the strip mill's concrete foundation had been poured over top of.[28] Machine foundations, tunnels, and basement walls were also discovered below ground. "It was unbelievable how many tunnels and underground structures there were," recalled Lee Gevaudan, RIDC director of development at the time. "Under the J&L mill buildings from the Hot Metal Bridge down, there was an extensive area of tunnels. When we got down there to look at them, there were crates and crates of food packets and water in large barrels still stored there. They were going to be used as air raid shelters during World War II."

New sewer lines, electric lines, and roads had to be laid. Between 7 and 10 feet of fill were needed to top off the 48-acre site, a considerable expense. Acting on RIDC's suggestion, the URA diverted all of the unwanted fill it excavated from its other projects throughout the city to the Technology Center to save money. The final cost of developing the site would reach $104 million.

Delays on and off the site prevented the partners from constructing a building or two in short order to showcase the new development and attract early tenants to demonstrate there was a market for the park—a strategy RIDC had successfully deployed at its suburban industrial parks. Once the environmental issues were resolved, however, development gained momentum and began earning at a pace that allowed for $7.5 million in tax increment financing obtained to help finance the project to be repaid 12 years early.[29] The first tenant, the University of Pittsburgh Center for Biotechnology and Bioengineering, opened in 1993. The first private company was recruited two years later, when RIDC built a regional headquarters for Union Switch & Signal Corporation to house its research and engineering departments. Other companies and institutions would settle there in the years to come, including Carnegie Mellon's Entertainment Technology Center, the Pittsburgh Technology Council, Catalyst Connection, Cellomics, which was eventually acquired by Thermo Fisher, Braskem, and Hitachi Rail STS, which acquired the company that had originally been Union Switch & Signal.

In redeveloping the former J&L Steel Company strip mill, RIDC proved to state and local government officials, and to itself, that it could navigate the challenges encountered when trying to turn industrial brownfields into places of new jobs and promise. The experience and confidence gained would further draw the nonprofit into the fraught debate over what to do about the shuttered steel mills and manufacturing plants multiplying throughout the region and the economic decline of the industrial suburbs they once supported.

Focus on the Mon Valley

RIDC found itself in the public spotlight it had tried to avoid for 35 years in the fall of 1991. It entered the new decade defending its practices in the local newspapers and before the Pennsylvania House of Representatives. Tom Murphy, a Democratic state representative from the North Side of Pittsburgh, accused it of unfairly using public money to lure companies out of the city to its suburban industrial parks. His concern for the city's competitiveness was grounded in the circumstances that enveloped it. Pittsburgh was hemorrhaging people, employers, and jobs. The city had lost 307,000 residents from 1950 to 1990—more than 45 percent of its population.[1] Such losses made it increasingly difficult to finance a higher level of services than was warranted by its population, which the city was obligated to provide as the center of commerce, employment, and entertainment in the region. Some residents had left southwestern Pennsylvania altogether to find jobs that were becoming scarce at home. Others left for the suburbs. New highways that made commuting less arduous encouraged the migration. As Pittsburgh was shrinking, for example, Cranberry Township in Butler County, the once-sleepy exurb where RIDC built its Thorn Hill industrial park, saw its population triple in size following the completion of Interstate 79, a four-lane throughway that connected it to the city.

Murphy first made the charges in an opinion article published in *The Pittsburgh Press*, the city's most-read daily newspaper. He returned to them a week later in hearings into nonprofit industrial development corporations—of which RIDC was one—that were conducted by a select committee of the state House, which he chaired. To illustrate his point, Murphy recounted how during the last six months of 1990, three Pittsburgh-based companies moved out of the city in favor of RIDC Park West near the Greater Pittsburgh International Airport. He complained that RIDC's access to low-interest Pennsylvania Industrial Development Authority financing that private developers could not get at the time allowed it to dangle lower-than-market-rate rent and purchase prices for its buildings to entice companies to its industrial parks. The three companies paid about one-third of the market rate per acre, Murphy wrote. "Why? RIDC has received public funds—in some cases millions of dollars—to develop its industrial parks. Clearly, something is wrong."[2]

The legislator conceded "RIDC has played a significant role in expanding our economy, providing homes for many corporations," and it had "contributed much to our regional growth." But most of the companies in the industrial parks had relocated from other parts of Allegheny County or the region, not from other states, Murphy pointed out. The parks they moved to were located in thriving suburban communities, not distressed municipalities desperate for an economic lifeline that were the concern of lawmakers who passed legislation establishing PIDA as a means of stimulating job growth in 1956.[3] "It is my contention that RIDC's current practices not only defeat the legislative intent, they also interfere with the growth of key areas, notably city neighborhoods and the Mon Valley, which must maintain their labor and tax base if the city and the region are to remain economically viable."

Not mentioned in the op-ed article was that the first building at the Pittsburgh Technology Center was about to open on a former steel mill brownfield in the city that RIDC and the city's Urban Redevelopment Authority worked together to reclaim; or that RIDC four years earlier had built a home in the city for the Software Engineering Institute, a major federally funded research center at Carnegie Mellon University; or that RIDC had secured PIDA loans to finance three University Technology Development Centers built in the city to incubate the ideas of researchers as potential businesses. Or that the Software Engineering Institute and the three technology development centers were built in the university-rich Oakland neighborhood, one of the city's hottest real estate markets. The op-ed article also neglected to mention that RIDC had acquired, at considerable financial risk, an enormous Westinghouse Electric Company factory complex that had recently closed east of the city and two shuttered steelworks in the Mon Valley, hoping to return jobs and investment to the distressed communities in which they were located.

Frank Brooks Robinson defended the development of RIDC's industrial parks before the House Select Committee Investigating Industrial Development Corporations, explaining that the nonprofit was asked by Allegheny County Commissioners to take over the county workhouse in suburban O'Hara Township that the officials wanted to close and turn into an industrial park. At Park West, few private developers were interested in developing the former Westinghouse property, even though it was close to the airport. The land had been strip-mined, a railroad scrapyard blighted its entrance, and it lacked utilities and other essential infrastructure. He described RIDC as "a risk taker investing in the development of properties long before private development interests paid any attention." Only after the industrial parks became successful did "private developers object about the unfair advantages enjoyed by RIDC."[4]

Furthermore, RIDC did not "try to convince companies to relocate from one county or region in our service area to another," Robinson testified. As to the complaint that companies were relocating in suburban industrial parks, not distressed communities, he argued RIDC could not force them to move to places where they did not want to move.[5]

The editorial board of the *Pittsburgh Post-Gazette* weighed in following the House committee's first hearing. It acknowledged that Murphy and other critics had raised important public-policy questions; that "it makes sense" that state funds should not be used to compete with private developers or move successful companies from one part of the region to another, or put industrial parks in "booming suburbs while development goes begging in economically struggling towns." However, "the difficulty comes in drawing bright lines in the law that would set development priorities for agencies like RIDC," which the newspaper believed had "performed admirably in fostering development for the past 35 years." The paper wondered whether using public money to "steal" a company from Cranberry and move it to the more needy North Side of Pittsburgh would be considered legitimate, before declaring, "the *Post-Gazette* continues to support the economic-development strategy of RIDC."[6]

Changes to PIDA would later follow, including a loosening of eligibility requirements so that industrial development agencies like RIDC no longer had near-exclusive access to attractive low-interest state loans. Policy changes within RIDC came more swiftly.

Having to testify before the House select committee left Robinson frustrated. But the experience gave him pause to reflect. Two months after the hearings, he told his board RIDC would have a new policy for dealing with company relocations, particularly from the City of Pittsburgh. RIDC would notify the city whenever a Pittsburgh-based business approaches it for help relocating out of the city. RIDC would then pause its relocation efforts for 60 days to allow the city to work with the company and try to convince it to stay. If the company still wanted to leave, RIDC would work to accommodate it. The policy, he said, had been favorably received by the city's URA. Robinson also recommended that the executive director of the URA have a seat on the RIDC board of directors.[7]

Robinson also reconsidered how RIDC was perceived by the Pittsburgh community. Getting entangled in contentious political controversies risked damaging the state and local contacts it had acquired over the years—contacts whose influence and resources had been critical to what it had accomplished and what it hoped to accomplish in the future. RIDC "will try to be more open about its activities," he told the board. It had been the policy of RIDC to maintain a low profile, but it was apparent the "profile has been too low." He was launching what he described as a "low-key general awareness" program. He would "work quietly" with the news media in order to provide, among other things, public announcements of RIDC projects.[8]

THE PLANT THAT ELECTRIFIED AMERICA

The historic Westinghouse Electric Corporation East Pittsburgh works was one of G. Reynolds Clark's first stops after he was hired as a young projectionist in the company's audio-visual department in 1966. It was a massive manufacturing complex, occupying an area roughly equivalent to 70 football fields about 10 miles east of Downtown Pittsburgh along Turtle Creek, a tributary of the Monongahela River. At its peak, it employed 22,000 workers. Its legacy was nothing less than being the manufacturing powerhouse behind the electrification of America. Clark was sent there for the physical examination the company required of its new employees. "You went to East Pittsburgh because there was a full-time hospital in the plant," he recalled. "They even had a maternity ward there for the wives of the workers. They had their own fire department." Twenty-four years later, he was the last Westinghouse employee out the door.

The plant opened in September 1894, only seven months after construction began, as a major expansion of the Westinghouse Electric & Manufacturing Company, which was the latest venture of George Westinghouse, one of the nation's most prolific inventors and influential entrepreneurs. More than two decades earlier, as a 22-year-old engineer with little formal education, he had invented a compressed-air railroad braking system that had taken the industry by storm. Now, he raced to gain a foothold in the generation of electricity, an industry with tremendous potential but still in its infancy. With profits from his Westinghouse Air Brake Company's factory in the Borough of Turtle Creek, he built a new plant a few miles downstream in East Pittsburgh as the flagship of his campaign to win what became known as the "War of the Currents."

The "war" was a bare-knuckle competition to decide which of two incompatible systems for distributing electricity to U.S. households and businesses would become the standard. Thomas Edison, inventor of the first practical lightbulb, and his supporters, who included powerful New York banker J.P. Morgan, promoted direct current. Direct current was more established at the time, but it could not be transmitted too far from the coal-fired generating stations that produced it. Westinghouse placed his bet on alternating current, which at high voltages could travel great distances but had to be stepped down to lower voltages to be used. He hired visionary engineer Nicola Tesla, an alternating current pioneer, and began making generators, transformers, and other equipment that alternating current required at the East Pittsburgh plant. Edison, a ruthless competitor, launched a misinformation campaign that attempted to define alternating current as dangerous for public use, going as far as to convince New York state corrections officials to use a Westinghouse generator in its first execution by electric chair to prove his point. Such efforts failed to have the effect Edison desired. Westinghouse won the contract to light the Chicago World's Fair with alternating current in 1893 and the exhibition dazzled. The same year, he won a contract to provide alternating current generators for the new hydroelectric power station at Niagara Falls in New York. The War of the Currents effectively came to an end in 1896 when the Niagara station lighted the city of Buffalo 26 miles away. Alternating current would power America. Business at Westinghouse's East Pittsburgh plant boomed.

George Westinghouse opened his East Pittsburgh plant for the Westinghouse Air Brake Company in 1894 and gradually added factories for the Westinghouse Electric & Manufacturing Company and the Westinghouse Machine Company. The 40-acre site included a machine shop, warehouse, powerhouse, brass foundry, punching and blacksmith shops, employed as many as 20,000 people, and was also the site of the first radio broadcast.

Now called Keystone Commons, RIDC transformed the complex into a home for more than 40 companies and it is considered one of the most successful redevelopment projects in the Commonwealth of Pennsylvania. Pictured here are (bottom left) George Westinghouse standing atop a huge turbine in the plant's West Shop, (top right) that same building as it is today—a multi-tenant facility that honors the past while providing modern space to companies—and (bottom right) an aerial view of the entire site.

All aspects of alternating current were manufactured in East Pittsburgh: turbine generator sets so big they had to be transported by two separate rail cars, transformers, switch gear, distribution equipment, even the meters that tracked the power usage of customers. Motors for the railroads and street cars were among the other products made in the numerous shops within the East Pittsburgh works. The plant was characterized by sturdy buildings of concrete, brick, and steel. Heavy manufacturing was done in structures with wide aisles, towering bays, and traveling cranes capable of lifting 30–50 tons. When the works had consumed nearly all of the 92-acre site, Westinghouse expanded upward, building a six-story "factory in the sky" at one end of the plant's West Shop and installing an elevator powerful enough to hoist railcars up to the top floors. The works had rail lines running through it, a machine shop, warehouses, brass foundry, blacksmith shops, office buildings, a library, recreational rooms for workers, and its own power plant.[9] "It was a city within the town of East Pittsburgh," Clark said.

The plant's legacy also includes an event unrelated to manufacturing: it was the site of the nation's first commercial radio broadcast. Westinghouse Electric saw the potential of radio early in the 20th century when few people owned receivers, the use of which was limited to communicating with other enthusiasts. Westinghouse officials believed a way to create a market for radio receivers was to heighten their appeal by having regularly scheduled broadcasts on a range of topics. The company established a radio station, KDKA, in 1920 and built a wooden shack to serve as a studio on the roof of one of the buildings in the East Pittsburgh works with an antenna and 100-watt transmitter. On November 2, 1920, KDKA made its first broadcast, reporting the results of the presidential election between Republican Warren Harding and Democrat James Cox as the numbers rolled in.[10]

Following World War II, the business empire George Westinghouse built from his airbrake plant expanded its interests to include rail, aviation, consumer appliances, and nuclear power. The company had plants across the country. Its Pittsburgh-based engineers were major contributors to the development of the nation's first fleet of nuclear-powered submarines. The company became an innovator and manufacturer

of commercial nuclear energy technology and management. But the
company would encounter serious financial setbacks, including heavy
losses in its credit division and declining sales and losses in its nuclear
power business, particularly after the 1979 nuclear reactor accident
at the Three Mile Island power plant near Harrisburg, Pennsylvania.
As its interests in television and radio broadcasting became a focus,
the company began to divest its consumer businesses and non-nuclear
manufacturing, selling divisions and companies piece by piece. By the
mid-1980s, it had little use for the East Pittsburgh works that had been
critical to its victory in the War of the Currents and was accepting
offers for its purchase.

~

On August 25, 1987, a special session of the executive committee of
the RIDC board of directors was called at the nonprofit's offices in
the Union Trust Building in Downtown Pittsburgh. Board chairman
Charles W. Parry and Robinson "wished to seek guidance" on the notion
of purchasing and redeveloping the Westinghouse East Pittsburgh plant.
In fact, Robinson had already given Westinghouse a proposal, which the
company was considering.

Robinson described the nearly 93-year-old plant as having been
"beautifully maintained." He worried about the prospect of it being sold
to a buyer more interested in cannibalizing the site for quick profit than
investing in the risky proposition of redeveloping it as a job-producing
industrial park. Westinghouse management was receptive to the idea
of local ownership, recalled Clark, who had risen from projectionist to
the executive ranks of the company. That was also the sense Robinson
took away from his meeting with Westinghouse chairman and chief
executive officer Douglas Danforth. Two years earlier, Danforth had led
a public-private coalition that was successful in buying the Pittsburgh
Pirates major league baseball franchise when it was up for sale, prevent-
ing it from being moved to another city at a time when the economically
battered region could ill afford another setback. Robinson proposed
that RIDC buy the property for $15 million to be paid over 15 years.
Redevelopment would be done in six phases during that window.

RIDC's responsibility for taxes and other property costs would be staggered. Westinghouse would continue to pay the costs on property RIDC had not yet developed, gradually ceding that responsibility to RIDC for each portion of the site it finished developing.[11] Danforth was in agreement, as long as the purchase price was firm. A private developer had also offered $15 million.

The decision whether to purchase the Westinghouse plant was cloaked in uncertainty. It was an industrial relic and, at 92 acres and 4.2 million square feet of total floor space under roof, a huge one at that. The extent of environmental remediation necessary was unknown. Robinson told the board that RIDC's ability to redevelop the site within the proposed 15-year time frame would depend a great deal on how quickly a sufficient market for the rehabbed buildings could be established, which would likely be a challenge given the depressed economic conditions in the Turtle Creek and Mon valleys. Furthermore, it was unclear how much support RIDC could expect from state and local government to ease the financial burden of redeveloping the plant. Parry, who was the chairman and chief executive officer of Alcoa, noted that a private developer would not have access to low-cost government financing that would be available to RIDC, and concluded that "the probability of a successful development favors RIDC." He told his board colleagues that he first viewed the Westinghouse plant negatively but had come around to thinking it represented the best opportunity of the three brownfield redevelopment projects RIDC was exploring, the other two being U.S. Steel's National Tube Works in McKeesport and its Duquesne works.

Parry echoed other board members' concerns over RIDC's obligation to meet the purchase price, which "could reduce RIDC's resources that otherwise would be available for seed funds." In other words, it could limit RIDC's ability to undertake future development projects. "It is a little bit like betting the entire farm since the net worth of RIDC is about equal to the cost," former RIDC president Hiram Milton said. Board member Leo Short, chairman of Mine Safety Appliances, asked whether "RIDC has ever put all of its eggs in one basket." J. David Barnes, chairman and CEO of Mellon Bank, said that if someone else was willing "to hassle with older buildings," RIDC should steer clear of them and stick to working with modern facilities. "Perhaps the old high-bay buildings have some reuse value, but what is the best use of RIDC's resources?" Robinson responded, saying he "desired to structure the purchase without selling the store." Expanding the time frame for meeting the purchase price to 20 years or even 25 years would reduce the risk, giving RIDC more time to secure grants and low-interest loans. He would negotiate with Westinghouse. Parry would speak with Danforth.

One year later, the board approved the purchase of the East Pittsburgh plant. Negotiations succeeded in lowering the price to $11.6 million with payment to be made over 25 years. Annual operating costs for taxes, insurance, debt service, security, and maintenance were estimated at $2.2 million. "This will create a significant cash responsibility for [RIDC]," Robinson said, "but one not unlike our initial undertaking to build an industrial park on undeveloped land [in suburban O'Hara Township], though the challenge will be greater because it is in a distressed urban area." The historic Westinghouse Electric & Manufacturing Company's East Pittsburgh works would have a new owner, a new purpose, and a new name: Keystone Commons.[12]

$$\sim$$

Keystone Commons was the second brownfield redevelopment under-taken by RIDC and the largest. The nonprofit was still learning about the challenges and pitfalls developers can expect when attempting to convert old industrial works to sites attractive to modern companies and wrestle with remediating them to new sets of environmental regulations that were being enacted. "We were naïve at the time," recalled Lee Gevaudan, RIDC's director of development when work was begun at Keystone Commons in 1989. "It turned out to be a money drain reme-diating down there. Back when that was built, asbestos was used for everything. You can't imagine how much asbestos was taken out of those facilities. Some of the structures had wooden flooring and underneath that was asbestos. All of that hardwood had to be taken up to get at the asbestos."

Another major undertaking was reconfiguring the utilities. The East Pittsburgh works had built and operated its own electric power generating station. RIDC's industrial park plan required abandoning the onsite generating station and rewiring the entire East Pittsburgh Works to allow power to be distributed to individual parcels and metered to determine each tenant's usage. Although the site had rail lines—even running through industrial buildings, in some cases—it did not have public roads for vehicles to conveniently access all of the shops on its sprawling footprint, which RIDC had to build and maintain.

What the East Pittsburgh works did have were sturdy, well-maintained buildings, many fortified with brick and concrete that had stood the test of time much better than local steel mills, which were constructed mostly of steel and had degraded to rusting hulks. Many of the original structures were kept and rehabbed. The complex offered options for tenants, ranging from 3,000 square feet to 100,000 square feet or larger and spaces suitable for offices or high-bay light industrial. The reimagined West Machine Shop became the most popular space within the former Westinghouse works. The cavernous shop had 500,000 square feet of floor space, a vaulted ceiling, and stood two stories high. Silent industrial films dating to 1904 show the frenetic pace of a factory teeming with workers whose labor was exhaustingly physical and who wore no protective gear as engines and heavy parts machinery traveled overhead on cranes and supervisors walked the floor in three-piece suits and bowler hats.

"The first time I walked in there it looked like a cross section of a gothic cathedral," Robinson recalled. It was the inspiration for converting the West Shop into an "industrial mall" designed for emerging companies looking to expand their operations. The central factory floor running the entire length of the shop was broad enough for indoor employee parking on both sides with enough room left for a tractor-trailer truck to pass through. Along each side of the shop, storefronts were built as the main entrance to tenant companies. Each storefront offered front office space, which opened to factory space in the back. On the second floor, storefront entrances were made accessible with stairways and elevators and a mall-like balcony walkway. "We froze one of the cranes midway so that there was a bridge that you get to both sides, what I called the monk's walk," Robinson said. "Then, we put elevators on both sides capable of lifting an automobile to the second floor."

The West Shop Industrial Mall was the showcase visited by companies being recruited to Keystone Commons during the early years when RIDC was trying to establish a market in the wake of recessions and the collapse of the southwestern Pennsylvania manufacturing economy. Relationships built years earlier with contractors helped prime the pump. "In the process of developing the greenfield sites, we got to know a lot of people in the contracting and subcontracting world. Many of them were based in the Mon Valley," Robinson recalled. "They had developed around the steel mills, or from them. I talked to a couple of these guys and they would say, 'You're never going to get me to move from the Mon Valley to O'Hara Township or, God help me, all the way out to Thorn Hill. Why aren't you doing something in the Mon Valley?' When we developed the industrial mall, they were the first one who came in—electrical contractors, plumbing, carpentry shops. Then, they'd bring in their buddies. Word of mouth goes out that they could get space there inexpensively. All of the little spaces had cranes in them. Anybody who had anything heavy to lift had their own crane to operate."

If the West Shop Industrial Mall was the most popular property at the former East Pittsburgh works, the six-story "factory in the sky" was the least. Modern manufacturing companies had little interest in stacking their operations vertically. One temporary tenant, however, earned Keystone Commons an obscure footnote in motion picture history. Producers of the 1991 thriller, *Silence of the Lambs*, leased a portion of the vertical factory, where they constructed a stone dry well portrayed in the film as part of the cavernous basement of serial killer "Buffalo Bill's" Belvedere, Ohio, home, in which he kept his soon-to-become-victims hostage.[13] That brought actress Jodie Foster to Keystone Commons as an FBI agent who rescues a hostage from the well. The film won Academy Awards for best picture, director, actress, actor, and screenplay.

Within three years of beginning the redevelopment of Keystone Commons, RIDC had leased space to 43 companies, which employed nearly 600 people. Robinson described the early outcomes as "remarkable progress in a soft market."[14] The industrial park was not yet generating enough income to cover the costs of operating it, however, and the losses were beginning to weigh on RIDC's bottom line. Recruiting more tenants couldn't come soon enough.

IN THE RED

Robinson's report of "remarkable progress" being made in signing tenants at Keystone Commons did little to assuage RIDC board members concerned about the nonprofit's finances. They had been warned that patience would be required to turn around such a large industrial plant, fill it with rent-paying tenants, and attract buyers for other parcels. What was not anticipated was that the United States, having endured a recession in the 1970s and two in the 1980s, would slip into yet another in 1990. Many businesses retrenched. Interest in expansion slowed. Leasing became a buyer's market. Growth in rental income slowed. RIDC lost tenants, eroding revenues further.

RIDC's debt more than doubled from 1988 to 1990. Paying the debt was constricting cash flow. As working capital began to shrink, so too did RIDC's ability to go forward with new projects. In May 1992, controller David Myron reported that RIDC's balance sheet showed very little liquidity. RIDC would likely have to draw on its $1 million line of credit to pay property taxes in August, and he expected the nonprofit to post a loss at the end of the year.[15] A special meeting of the board was called in July to review RIDC's financial condition and discuss a recovery strategy. Myron broadly outlined steps that had to be taken for RIDC to recover. Rental income, its major source of revenue, was flat due to the depressed real estate market and had to improve. Occupancy rates had to rise. Only 20 percent of Keystone Commons properties were occupied. Across the rest of RIDC's portfolio, 70 percent of properties were occupied. Debt levels had to be reduced to more manageable levels. RIDC would have to reduce the level of future property, buildings, and equipment investments. Operating expenses had to trimmed, including the possibility of laying off staff and moving RIDC offices to facilities it owned.[16]

Leases had already been revised to reduce RIDC's costs. Recent leases and, until further notice, future leases would require tenants to finance any building modification or improvement they may want— something RIDC had paid for in the past. Tenants who chose to do so would receive a reduction in their rent as compensation. Leasehold improvement clauses, however, were a double-edged sword. While they would lower RIDC's costs, they risked having a chilling effect on attracting tenants, particularly small and young companies with limited resources. Robinson also asked the Pennsylvania Industrial Development Authority to allow RIDC to pay only the interest on its PIDA loans for the time being to lower its debt service. Negotiations to restructure some commercial loans would begin. Trimming of operating costs began the following month, when six of RIDC's 21 employees were laid off.

Investments, cash, and cash flow continued to decline the following year. But there were signs that the recovery strategy was easing the financial crisis, at least slightly. Capital expenses were down and more debt was being paid than new money borrowed. Keystone was still posting an operating loss, but the losses were shrinking. Occupancy had increased. It had edged up to 24 percent at Keystone Commons. Still, board member Barnes argued, with 85 percent of RIDC's other properties occupied, it was clear Keystone Commons continued to be a considerable drag on finances. He suggested RIDC either "let go of Keystone Commons" or find some way to accelerate the recruitment of tenants and increase rentals.[17] It would not be the last time Robinson would hear suggestions that RIDC should abandon its brownfield redevelopments in the economically distressed industrial corridors of southwestern Pennsylvania.

Robinson resisted suggestions to "let go" of Keystone Commons. He believed more tenants would be added and income would increase, telling the board if all went well the industrial park could break even on a cash basis by the end of 1994. RIDC's investment in the project, including commercial and PIDA loans and equity, totaled $36 million by then. RIDC's losses had risen to $8 million, a sum it expected to recover from future earnings.[18] It would take nearly the rest of the 1990s for Keystone Commons to break even. Ten years after RIDC acquired the former Westinghouse works, 60 percent of the site was occupied by 55 companies, ranging from a manufacturer of galvanized sheet to a commercial bakery, and an estimated 1,500 people worked there.[19] Progress would be even slower at the two shuttered steelworks the nonprofit was redeveloping in the Mon Valley cities of McKeesport and Duquesne.

Liability Concerns

Recycling old industrial sites was an emerging field when RIDC agreed to take on the redevelopment of the former U.S. Steel McKeesport National Tube Works and its Duquesne works on the other side of the Monongahela River. There were a number of unsettled issues, not the least of which was how to deal with the legacy of environmental contamination that came with them. Environmental regulation related to industrial sites was in the early stages of development in the 1980s with new laws and rules being written by state legislators and federal agencies. Of particular concern to RIDC and other developers looking at turning industrial brownfields into something useful again was the extent of their liability for environmental insults committed by previous owners over decades during which they were not held responsible for managing hazardous waste. "When we started at McKeesport and Duquesne, I was worried about liability," Robinson recalled. "I had gone to my attorney and asked, how do I protect my estate from being liquidated because somebody had done something stupid and it came down the line to me."

The Allegheny County Industrial Development Authority negotiated with U.S. Steel to take title to the McKeesport and Duquesne steelworks in 1988, and RIDC—only months after signing the deal to buy the Westinghouse plant in East Pittsburgh—agreed to remediate and market the mill sites for the county. Two years later, RIDC would take ownership of the McKeesport and Duquesne mills. The National Tube Works, incorporated in 1869, was at one time the largest producer of steel pipe in the world. The Duquesne works, which fired its first furnace in 1886, produced semi-finished steel with Bessemer converters, open hearth, and electric basic oxygen processes. Taking an environmentally sensitive approach to disposing of unwanted equipment and industrial waste had not been the strong suit of the steelworks for most of their operational life. Nor had it been a concern of government until the 1950s. Even then, early regulations were lenient compared to later standards.

RIDC knew from its experience redeveloping the former Jones & Laughlin Steel Company Pittsburgh Works to expect surprises beneath the surface of old steel mill sites. Company records were often of little help. "Sometimes, we would run into someone who had worked at the site and they would mention some of the problems," RIDC's Gevaudan recalled. "[The company] had extensive files and drawings, but there weren't any updated ones—nothing to say this is what was on the site then and this is what is here now. It was a hodgepodge of plans from way, way back." At Duquesne, for example, a landscaping crew discovered a buried rail car and had to use jackhammers to plant trees.[20] At McKeesport, "we started extending the road and in the space of about 1,000 feet we ran into 14–15 tanks filled with everything from oil and lubricants to the finish they put on the tubing to keep it from rusting," Gevaudan said. A blast furnace at McKeesport presented another issue. "When they stopped operations there, they did it so quickly that there was a chunk of metal left in the oven. When the building around it was demolished, there was this big chunk of metal. We never were able to take it out. What we did was change the grades there so we could build over it."

RIDC ordered environmental assessments of the two former steelworks. But with regulations still in flux, the nonprofit was unsure what its liability risk would be, regardless of what the assessments found and what was done to remediate it. Regulating industrial waste management and remediation had intensified after the 1980 Comprehensive Environmental Response, Compensation, and Liability Act, commonly known as the Superfund legislation, was enacted by Congress in the wake of the Love Canal environmental disaster, which linked the deaths and illnesses of a wide swath of residents to a company's decades-long practice of dumping and burying toxic chemicals in the small western New York town. The federal law established prohibitions and requirements concerning closed and abandoned hazardous waste sites, fixed liability to those responsible for hazardous waste, and established a trust fund to finance the cleanup when no responsible party could be identified.

States also had a role in defining how hazardous waste was to be managed and remediated within their borders. In Pennsylvania, local officials complained the redevelopment of abandoned industrial sites was being discouraged by state Department of Environmental Resources practices, which often insisted the sites be cleaned up to their natural state, or to pre-industrial "background," a standard developers argued was extreme and often unnecessary to protect the public, and cost-prohibitive, in most cases. "I sat in many meetings where there were reasonable discussions about how to address an issue, but it always came back to, 'No, you have to clean it up to background,'" recalled Mark Urbassik, who co-founded KU Resources, an environmental consulting firm with experience in brownfield redevelopment projects dating to the first ones attempted in southwestern Pennsylvania.

The Duquesne steelworks, along with the Homestead and Edgar Thomson works, all built in the Pittsburgh region in the late 19th century, propelled Andrew Carnegie and his company, U.S. Steel, to the top of the steel industry. It began production in 1889 with a new process for rolling rails and soon added a 12-furnace open hearth steel plant that produced 50-ton heats of steel up to three times each day (bottom left). Credit: Rivers of Steel

After shutting down in 1984, the property stood dormant and quickly deteriorated (top right). Allegheny County asked RIDC to clean up and redevelop the 240-acre site, which now—in buildings recognizable by their distinctive green metal roofs and known as City Center of Duquesne—includes a diverse array of 15 companies, employing hundreds of people (bottom right).

Moreover, the state lacked clear, predictable environmental remediation standards and a process for developing those standards. Urbassik described the mid-1980s to mid-1990s as "a decade of confusion" over how to regulate brownfield redevelopment in Pennsylvania. "What developers kept telling the [Department of Environmental Resources] at the time was, 'tell me what I need to do.' The problem was the uncertainty. 'Give me my target so I know what I need to do.' They had no way to estimate a cost. There was no certainty with transfers of previously used property." Liability was borne by the new owners of a shuttered industrial plant, as well as future owners. The uncertainty and liability risks were more reasons for already leery investors to avoid former mill sites. "The lawyers wouldn't let you touch some of the properties," Urbassik recalled.

Within two years of agreeing to buy the former McKeesport and Duquesne steelworks, RIDC had spent $16 million—roughly $34 million in 2024 dollars—to remove asbestos, oils, highly carcinogenic polychlorinated biphenyls, and other hazardous materials identified in the environmental assessments it had ordered. Yet, the nonprofit's liability risk remained unclear. Heightening RIDC's concern was what Robinson felt was an antagonistic attitude among DER staff, who he complained at a chamber of commerce luncheon in 1993 made surprise inspections and threatened to fine the nonprofit if it didn't pick up the pace of ridding the sites of hazardous materials that had been allowed to accumulate for more than a century before RIDC had taken ownership. While top DER officials, including the agency's secretary and regional director, had been cooperative, some staff of lower authority "still believe that industry is evil and that everybody is dragging their feet on the cleanup—which is what we all want."[21]

Robinson, who had returned to RIDC in 1981 after serving in former governor Dick Thornburgh's administration, took his argument for liability limits to the state capital. State and local officials were eager to clean up and redevelop the growing number of abandoned industrial sites for the benefit of the communities around them. He told the new governor, Tom Ridge, "If you want the brownfields to be redeveloped, somebody has got to provide protection for the undertaking of that," Robinson recalled. He then met with David Brightbill, the Lebanon County Republican who was majority leader in the state Senate. Brightbill had him work with his administrative aide in framing legislation that addressed the liability issues. RIDC's influence would be apparent in the Pennsylvania Land Recycling and Environmental Remediation Standards Act adopted in 1995.

The law—commonly referred to as "Act 2"—recognized that eliminating public health and environmental hazards on commercial and industrial land was "vital to their use and reuse as sources of employment, housing, recreation and open-space areas," and that it was necessary to encourage site development and cleanup "without the use of taxpayer funds or the need for adversarial enforcement actions by the Department of Environmental Resources, which frequently only serve to delay cleanups and increase their cost."[22] It defined a set of remediation standards lawmakers felt met the state's constitutional obligation to protect its citizens' right to "clean air, pure water, and to the preservation of the natural, scenic, historic and esthetic values of the environment,"[23] while giving developers the regulatory clarity they sought.

Folded into the act was a voluntary program that provided the liability protection that RIDC had advocated for. Site owners could earn liability relief if they complied with a remediation process that included conducting an environmental assessment and coming up with a plan to address any environmental problem that was found to the satisfaction of state regulators.[24] Liability relief was awarded only for the conditions identified in the assessment, underscoring the importance of conducting a thorough investigation. Once earned, liability relief could be transferred to future owners of the property, lessening the risk to new buyers, who had shied from investing in the depressed factory and mill towns that were emptying out across the state.

Former Pennsylvania governor Tom Ridge signed Act 2, which governs remediation of former industrial brownfields, at a ceremony at RIDC's Industrial Center of McKeesport in 1995.

MCKEESPORT AND DUQUESNE

Owning the U.S. Steelworks in McKeesport and Duquesne was not RIDC's intention when it agreed to help Allegheny County market the sites and prepare the land for redevelopment. The county had a deal with the company—renamed USX—to acquire the sites for $3.8 million to be paid over 20 years. Within three years, the county, looking to limit its involvement in the project, asked RIDC to take over. In 1990, a three-way deal was negotiated under which the sites were conveyed to RIDC, along with the county's obligation to pay USX the $3.8 million. The steelmaker would continue to pay the taxes on the land. As each acre was sold, the first $10,000 of the purchase price would go to USX as payment toward the debt RIDC owed. The next $20,000 would be paid to the development fund RIDC set up for the sites. Anything over $30,000 would be split evenly between the two.[25]

Taking on the steelworks in the Mon Valley worried the RIDC board of directors, particularly the banking executives. Robinson warned them the projects would require patience. They would be costly and the largesse of funding sources—mostly state agencies—could be fickle over time. Site preparation would be difficult. Act 2 environmental liability limits weren't enacted at the time the projects were proposed. The Mon Valley commercial real estate market was in tatters. RIDC's debt was mounting. But the county wanted RIDC to take over the projects, as did the Pennsylvania Industrial Development Authority, which had been born from discussions among lawmakers around revitalizing declining communities. And RIDC wanted to protect its relationship with PIDA, which had been the source of low-interest loans that fueled the non-profit's growth and would be critical to repurposing the mill sites.

"When we started, no private developer would even think about going down in either East Pittsburgh or the Mon Valley," Robinson recalled. "No bank would make a loan. These are discussions I had many times with [Dollar Bank Chairman] Steve Hanson and David Barnes, who was the head of Mellon Bank. Mellon Bank wasn't going to put any money down there. They don't take that kind of risk. But who does? He was a banker. His philosophy was, sell everything and turn it into capi-tal." Acquiring the Duquesne works as a package deal with McKeesport also raised red flags. Reiterating RIDC's mission helped bring reluctant members on board. Hansen was among them. "I had to say to him, 'When you're talking with me at RIDC, you have to put away your bank thinking and think community development. When I'm on your board at Dollar Bank and sit in your board meetings, I'm thinking only about the risk that would be taken on a loan. It's an entirely different thing.' Fortunately, Hanson understood that." The board approved the Mon Valley acquisitions but urged RIDC to move cautiously. Robinson understood that redeveloping the steelworks "weren't good financial moves. But if it didn't happen, they'd still be there in wretched shape."

Rising scrap metal prices provided a timely windfall for RIDC, which was encountering higher-than-expected remediation and develop-ment costs. By the end of 1995, U.S. scrap iron and steel was selling for nearly five times what it sold for in 1960.[26] Major buyers included U.S. mini-mills, which made steel from scrap rather than ore and were among the competitors whose modern processes contributed to the decline of the Mon Valley steelworks. Sales of scrap and equipment from the McKeesport and Duquesne works totaled upwards of $15 million by 1994[27] and would end up covering the cost of remediating the sites and preparing them for development.

Many of the steelmaking structures at Duquesne and McKeesport had not been well maintained. Robinson cynically described them as being "built to keep the rain off of the machinery." While the sturdier brick buildings—some dating to the 19th century—were rehabilitated, most steelmaking structures were razed after they had been cleaned of asbestos and other hazardous material. The exception was the Dorothy Six furnace at the Duquesne works. In negotiations with USX and Allegheny County, RIDC expressed interest in acquiring only the McKeesport steelworks. Overextending its resources was a concern with the Keystone Commons redevelopment already underway in East Pittsburgh. At 240 acres, the Duquesne works was nearly twice the size of the McKeesport steelworks. USX insisted, however, that Duquesne be part of the deal. Robinson relented, but insisted that the Dorothy Six blast furnace be excluded from the package. Dorothy Six was among the youngest furnaces in the company's inventory and the most advanced. In 1983, it set production records and steelworkers were awarded "Ironmaster" jackets to wear in recognition of the achievement.[28] The company announced it was closing the Duquesne works a few months later and had scheduled Dorothy Six for demolition. The announcement touched off angry protests and inspired a high-profile campaign by steelworkers and their supporters to save and reopen the blast furnace complex as an employee-owned operation, which included trying (unsuccessfully) to convince local municipalities to use eminent domain to seize it. Protests and political pressure managed to delay the razing of the blast furnace for years. Once considered "the crown jewel of the Mon Valley," Dorothy Six had become "a symbol of a community's fight against economic forces far beyond their control."[29] Robinson didn't want any part of that. "I told [USX], that's yours."

RIDC's approach to the mill sites—renamed the Industrial Center of McKeesport and the City Center of Duquesne—was similar to that which guided the establishment of its other industrial parks: take a property onsite and construct a building as soon as possible to attract a tenant and demonstrate the market. "We felt that somebody had to set the pace, set the example," Robinson recalled. "My feeling was that if we could just get a footprint down there the capital would follow it." Within two years of owning the McKeesport site, RIDC built one building and renovated another. A manufacturer of glossy aluminum-coated paper, the Metallized Paper Corporation of America was the first company to land at the new industrial park. A large call center followed. The City Center of Duquesne, which faced more complex remediation issues, developed at a slower pace. Urbassik and his partner opened their environmental consulting company there, finding it "a lot more affordable than trying to set up an office downtown." In the late 1990s, the Greater Pittsburgh Community Food Bank chose to build its new home at the Duquesne industrial park. Its building was the first Leadership in Energy and Environmental Design (LEED)-certified food bank in the United States and was large enough to accommodate the warehousing, preparation, and distribution of tens of millions of pounds of food each year. The food bank, which started during the height of steel layoffs in the 1980s, became the hub of hunger relief in southwestern Pennsylvania, providing more than 42 million meals a year to people in 11 counties.[30]

Both Mon Valley projects developed more slowly than RIDC's other industrial parks. When the nonprofit first considered the projects, it anticipated the proposed Mon-Fayette Expressway connecting West Virginia to Pittsburgh would greatly improve highway transportation to and from McKeesport and Duquesne, adding luster to the industrial parks in the eyes of companies looking for an affordable home. Three decades later, ground still hadn't been broken on the section of the expressway through those cities.[31] And development of the industrial parks did little to persuade private developers uninterested in the Mon Valley. "I would love to have a private interest come down here, buy five acres and build a building," Brooks Robinson Jr., son of the RIDC president and director of marketing for the nonprofit's Mon Valley sites, told the *Pittsburgh Post-Gazette*. "It would be great. It's upsetting me, because no one is down here." And RIDC had its own finances to consider. By 1999, it had $105 million in equity, loans, and grants invested in Keystone Commons, McKeesport, and Duquesne. As an organization, it was carrying $140 million in debt, including $45 million in loan obligations to PIDA.[32] Limited by costs, lack of interest, and its own precarious finances, RIDC worked cautiously in McKeesport and Duquesne, mostly developing parcels only where there were signs of interest.

The political and social terrain in the Mon Valley was different and more challenging than in any of the other places in the region where RIDC had undertaken development projects. When RIDC first arrived, hope that the steel industry would rebound was still in the air. The notion RIDC was going to raze steelmaking structures threatened those hopes. Robinson recalled having conversations about that with members of the Duquesne city council. "It was made up of older gentlemen who had been steelworkers and they were bitter. They weren't angry with me. They were angry with U.S. Steel. But they were skeptical: Why did I come in? If I had not come in, they thought that steel might come back. I knew, and I think they knew, that wasn't going to happen. I would say to them, I'm not down here as a social worker. Anything we do here as a way of creating employment isn't going to help you. It may not help your children. But it will help the generation that follows. That's a tough sell. Many of these guys had been steelworkers all of their lives. I had to somehow keep that anger from infecting what we were trying to do down there." It didn't help that companies and jobs were slow to come. Nine years after RIDC took ownership, the industrial parks had brought 1,500 new jobs to McKeesport, but only 400 to Duquesne.

Several decades would pass before the Industrial Center of McKeesport and the City Center of Duquesne would break even on the balance sheet. The idea that once RIDC began building on the former steel sites private capital would follow turned out to be overly optimistic, despite the incentives of low rent and below-market real estate prices and municipalities eager to welcome and work with new employers. Distressed mill towns in the Mon Valley and elsewhere would continue to be seen as forsaken places too risky for investment well into the next century. In 2023, looking back on his long career at RIDC, Robinson recalled with regret the lack of interest in the Mon Valley when it needed it the most. "If the private banking community didn't feel it was too risky . . . things would've happened more rapidly. The nature of the redevelopment in McKeesport and Duquesne likely would've changed."

University Strategy Takes Hold

Southwestern Pennsylvania's century-long relationship with steel would never be the same. Most of the largest steelworks in the region had closed or were being closed, and jobs that had sustained generations of steelworkers and their families were being eliminated along with them by 1988, when a group of architects and planners appeared at a public meeting in Homestead. Known as the Regional Urban Design Assistance Team, it had been assembled by the American Institute of Architects to study the Mon Valley and brainstorm ideas for reimagining the steelworks being abandoned with alarming frequency. On a cold Saturday morning in February, they gave residents a preview of the report they would present at an international Remaking Cities Conference in Downtown Pittsburgh the coming week. It didn't go well. It wasn't the lukewarm reception to their ideas that caught the architects and planners off guard. It was that so many of the estimated 100 people in the audience rejected the premise that the steelworks were closing for good.

"You have to move forward," New York City architect Michael Kwartler told them. "This is like a lingering divorce that, until it is finally settled, is very painful, and even after it is settled will be painful." Many in the audience who spoke, including Homestead mayor Betty Esper, argued it was premature to redevelop the mills—that there was still time for the slumping steel industry to bounce back. "You're going to have to face reality. They're gone," countered Tony McGann, a community planner from Liverpool, England, where industrial plants had also closed. "If you wait for steel to come back, you'll wait forever." Criticism that the study team was out of touch with the realities weighing on the mill towns rankled its chairman, John Clarke, a Trenton, New Jersey, architect and planner. "There is so much handwringing and concern that the team doesn't understand the economic hardships of the mills closing," he said. "But the team does understand that. The question is, where do we go from here?"[1]

It was a question that elsewhere in the region, government officials, universities, RIDC, and others had already answered as they began to steer southwestern Pennsylvania toward a new economy that emphasized exploiting innovations coming out of local research universities as a way to stimulate growth, diversity, and renewal. They had their work cut out for them. In 1962, RIDC had assembled some of the region's top scientists as a standing advisory group to identify opportunities for turning the ideas of researchers into products, companies, and jobs and to "prevent ideas with industrial development potential from leaving the area."[2] Later, it found homes for several young technology companies at lower-than-market-rate rent in its suburban industrial parks. But there was little support available to nurture entrepreneurs, no regionwide movement for accelerating the growth of a robust tech sector, or a strong commitment from the state to fund such an effort. It took the realization that an economic crisis like few others was upon them for momentum to build.

State government took a more forward-looking approach to economic development with the election of Dick Thornburgh as governor in 1978. Among the recommendations to come out of his Commission on Choices for Pennsylvanians was to develop policies that supported the growth of advanced technology as a key sector of the state economy. That led to establishing the Ben Franklin Partnership in 1982. The partnership created four advanced technology centers across the state to encourage greater cooperation between universities and the private sector on creating jobs through industrial modernization and technological innovation. Carnegie Mellon University and the University of Pittsburgh sponsored and managed the southwestern Pennsylvania center, where partners included businesses, economic development organizations, financial institutions, and others. Statewide, the program raised more than $750 million in state funding, along with matching private sector funds and contributions from universities during its first seven years. The money financed research and development projects in advanced materials, biotechnology, software, robotics, and other fields. The centers offered entrepreneurial development, and education and training.[3] "Times are tough around here. It's the need that is driving high technology. That's what makes the governor and mayor take notice," James Colker, president of Contraves Goertz Corporation, a leading technology firm in the region, told *The Pittsburgh Press*.[4]

A sense of urgency spread among government, academic, and civic leaders. A flurry of working groups, commissions, studies, and reports assessed the region's strengths, weaknesses, and opportunities to restore stability to the economy and lead the region toward prosperity. Among the earliest was Strategy 21. State representative Tom Murphy of Pittsburgh's North Side convinced city and Allegheny County officials in 1985 to consolidate their public and private capital funding requests and reach consensus on spending priorities, in part to support their case for more state funding after Philadelphia received up to $200 million for a convention center. The county asked Allegheny Conference on Community Development executive director Robert Pease to oversee a coalition to recommend spending priorities that included city and county government, the Pennsylvania Economy league, Carnegie Mellon, and the University of Pittsburgh. Within months, they delivered Strategy 21, which set broad goals and prioritized projects for state funding. The most expensive was a new terminal for the Greater Pittsburgh International Airport and the Southern Expressway, a highway proposed to improve Pittsburgh's connection to the airport and encourage development along that corridor. Funds were requested for the Pittsburgh Technology Center on the site of a shuttered steel mill in Pittsburgh's South Oakland neighborhood, which RIDC would soon help the city develop. And they identified building a supercomputer center and research centers for robotics, biotechnology, and software engineering as other priorities.[5]

Two years earlier, as regional unemployment rose above 16 percent, RIDC, Penn's Southwest and others had established the Pittsburgh Technology Council, one of the first organizations in the region to provide much-needed support to a budding technology sector, its entrepreneurs, and companies. While U.S. Steel was closing its Duquesne and American Bridge works, RIDC was negotiating with the City of Pittsburgh to define its role in building the Pittsburgh Technology Center as a new home for university researchers and technology companies. And as labor activists put fish in bank safe-deposit boxes to protest the reluctance to invest in the Mon Valley, RIDC was working with the University of Pittsburgh and Carnegie Mellon to build out an innovation corridor of research labs, centers, and companies that would extend beyond their campuses in the Oakland neighborhood of Pittsburgh.

With its first University Technology Development Center on Oakland's Henry Street, RIDC started addressing a gap in the crowded university corridor that had implications for the growth of the local technology sector. For small companies, which many local tech firms were, finding adequate and affordable office and lab space was a challenge. A century of steel and heavy manufacturing dominance had led to complacency in building a support structure for new industries that rise from ideas, entrepreneurs, and small companies. "It is difficult for small companies to exist concurrently with large, capital-intensive industries," said Colker, who served as the first president of the Pittsburgh Technology Council. Henry Street, a short walk from the Carnegie Mellon campus, soon became a coveted real estate market among tech firms. With Carnegie Mellon, RIDC built the University Technology Development Center in 1983 as an incubator for start-ups, offering flexible office and research space, and administrative and business services for entrepreneurs, who might find support to be as close as the next office over. The Pittsburgh office of the Ben Franklin Partnership program and the Pittsburgh Technology Council were among the first tenants. One year later, as the LTV Aliquippa works in Beaver County became the latest casualty of steel's decline, two-thirds of the University Technology Development Center was filled within months of its opening. RIDC started on a second center for the University of Pittsburgh to keep up with demand. A few years later, it would build a third.[6]

In RIDC, the universities found an experienced developer with patience and the willingness to act on the belief that technological innovation was a catalyst for economic recovery. "You need a partner who is going to be able to take a longer time horizon, put a community vision first, ahead of their own private development aspirations, but, more critically, to take the risk that there is going to be a future. Private developers take risks, but they take risks with the market being clear. At the time, it was not clear that market would grow," recalled Timothy McNulty, associate vice president for government relations at Carnegie Mellon University, who had served in the state Department of Community and Economic Development, including as its acting secretary.

Believing in the potential of the region's universities seemed a safer bet by the end of 1985. They had won national competitions in the span of 14 months that delivered two highly coveted technology centers to the region, giving civic and political leadership, in particular, a sense that the shift toward a more technology-focused economy was a goal the region could accomplish. A joint bid by Carnegie Mellon, the University of Pittsburgh, and the Westinghouse Electric Corporation was selected for one of five National Science Foundation supercomputing centers, giving university scientists access to the most powerful computers available at the time. Universities in Japan, France, Italy, and Germany were well stocked with supercomputers, but the ultra-fast machines were found at only four U.S. universities. Federal officials worried that the country's academic researchers were falling behind in the race to develop advanced technologies as a result. "You know there's a problem when a number of our university-based researchers have to go to France to run their programs," said U.S. representative Doug Walgren, a Democrat from Mt. Lebanon, who chaired the House Subcommittee on Research and Technology.[7] The other winning bid sent a clear signal the region was emerging as a national technology hub.

The U.S. Department of Defense decided a national institute was necessary to advance the development of computer software, a field essential to national defense systems—from intelligence gathering to missile guidance—that was rapidly growing in scale and complexity. A competition for the contract to host and manage a national Software Engineering Institute attracted proposals from the top computer schools in the nation. The Pentagon's announcement in November 1984 that Carnegie Mellon would be awarded the $103 million contract was immediately embraced as a lifeline for an economy in decline. It was seen as a major attraction for top software engineering talent that would expand the tech community and the number of companies in the region. "I really believe we're going to see some important changes in the economy as a result of this," Carnegie Mellon president Richard Cyert said.[8] "I see this thing snowballing and I don't think I'm being overly optimistic." The Pittsburgh Technology Council's Colker described it as a rare "watershed" of change.

RIDC began building the institute in Pittsburgh's Oakland neighborhood before Carnegie Mellon's contract to manage it was publicly announced. RIDC president Frank Brooks Robinson's remarks about its potential impact were optimistic, but measured, saying the institute "raises a signal to the country at large that Pittsburgh is emerging in this field," while pointing out that the institute and the kind of companies it would attract tend to rely on highly educated, specifically trained employees. "We still need to create job opportunities for people who might not fit into that kind of workforce."[9]

~

Most working-aged people in the region didn't fit into that kind of workforce. Many of them were leaving as steel and manufacturing jobs once considered dependable vanished and the region's job market shifted toward other sectors. Years of decline and the loss of 158,000 manufacturing jobs had devastating effects on the region's population. It led to an exodus the scale of which southwestern Pennsylvania had never experienced, posing a threat to its workforce, attractiveness to businesses, local government tax revenue, population-based state and federal funding, and representation in Harrisburg and Washington. The region lost more than 289,000 residents between 1970 and 1990. Young adults left in large numbers for jobs and career opportunities they did not find at home, and they took their future families with them. A Carnegie Mellon study estimated that people who left the region between 1970 and 2000 later had 205,000 children who were born elsewhere.[10] The loss of so much youth knocked the demographics of the region out of balance, skewing the population older and leading to natural population loss—more deaths than births in a year—for decades to come. "There was a desperation," recalled Timothy Parks, who served as president and chief executive officer of the Pittsburgh Technology Council and, later, the Pittsburgh Regional Alliance, an economic development marketing nonprofit. "The feeling was, it was not like having your finger in the dike; it was like water rushing past you and you couldn't stop it."[11]

Civic leaders worried such a population drain would leave the workforce short of the talent necessary to grow and sustain a new economy led by medicine, technology, and education that they saw gaining momentum with early success stories such as FORE Systems, a computer network equipment company founded in 1990 by four Carnegie Mellon University professors that started in the University Technology Development Center and quickly scaled up to 1,000 employees. The concern led to some eclectic marketing concepts aimed at restoring the young adult population. One was "Border Guard Bob," a fictional character to be featured in television ads in full uniform and campaign hat—think Smokey Bear—stopping young people at the border to convince them to stay in the region and attaching a bungee cord to the car of one who couldn't be persuaded, declaring: "He'll be back." A focus group loved it. But criticism that the ad made the region appear unflatteringly desperate led the Pittsburgh Regional Alliance to shelve it. Another short-lived campaign was the "mystery city" project. In that one, technology workers in California's Silicon Valley would be offered an all-expense paid trip to an undisclosed location described in terms that made it seem like heaven on earth. Only before boarding the plane would they be told it was Pittsburgh. But word leaked out, ruining the mystery, and, like Border Guard Bob, the project was abandoned. The lesson learned from such exercises was that marketing campaigns cannot engineer what it takes to convince people to move to or stay in the region. "There's no question jobs and opportunity are what attracts people. People usually don't move to a city just to try it out," Parks said. The exodus slowed and the population began to stabilize after 1990, when the economy steadily diversified and the region drew closer to what Parks described as a "multi-faceted landscape of opportunity."

CATCHING WAVES

Neither the Software Engineering Institute nor the Supercomputing Center generated the scale of economic activity their most vocal advocates had predicted. But each stood as clear evidence that the region had the resources to build a new economy. More importantly, their cachet contributed to the aggregation of talent, expertise, and capabilities, particularly within the universities. A key difference between the post-war renewal under the Renaissance programs and the movement to restore economic health in the wake of the catastrophic decline of the manufacturing base was the role of universities as economic catalysts, which they recognized and aggressively embraced. "We're interested in the economy," Carnegie Mellon's Cyert told the *Pittsburgh Post-Gazette*. "We think that you can't have a growing, vibrant national university in an environment that is decaying."[12]

More than anything, the awarding of the Software Engineering Institute and the Pittsburgh Supercomputing Center was validation that Carnegie Mellon and the University of Pittsburgh had risen to the top tier of American universities in terms of their research capabilities. "You can't just put in some research money and expect that you are going to generate economic impact," McNulty said. "It really does depend on establishing clear excellence in a field so you can draw the talent, draw investment from public and private sources and create a context for innovation to take place."

Both universities made significant investments in fields they believed they had the expertise to lead and from which innovations would emerge that had great commercial value. Carnegie Mellon focused on computer science and robotics. It had established one of the first academic computer science departments in the country in 1965. Cyert later oversaw the creation of a school of computer science. He launched Project Andrew with a $100 million investment from IBM, connecting all of the computers on campus to a single network. The distributed network, while common today, had never been done before. Six years after Carnegie Mellon won the Software Engineering Institute contract, Cyert secured funding from the Westinghouse Electric Corporation to establish the Robotics Institute, the first academic robotics department in the country, and created the first doctoral program in the field. Under Cyert's successor, Robert Mehrabian, the university determined that the field of mobile robotics had reached the point where commercial uses were possible and established the National Robotics Engineering Consortium in 1994 to both develop robotic technologies and to help companies and federal agencies adopt them. The willingness of university leadership to make big bets on nascent technologies, McNulty observed, "led to these big applied capabilities, especially in robotics, where [the school] not only does fundamental research, but does applied research and becomes a magnet to bring companies here and accelerate start-ups."

At the University of Pittsburgh, Chancellor Wesley Posvar focused on health sciences and biotechnology, fields in which it had already earned nation attention. Led by Jonas Salk, the school had played a leading role in developing the polio vaccine during the 1950s. Its medical researchers and surgeon Thomas Startz were pioneers in organ transplantation and the use of immunosuppressive drugs who helped advance transplantation from fantasy to a life-saving therapy for patients with heart, liver, and kidney diseases. The school invested in a new biotechnology research center, which became one of the first labs built at the Pittsburgh Technology Center on the reclaimed site of the former Jones & Laughlin steelworks. Posvar convinced Chevron to donate the former 53-building Gulf Oil research complex in Harmar Township east of the City of Pittsburgh, where the university opened the University of Pittsburgh Applied Research Center as home to several of its research initiatives, as well as those of more than 100 small companies. The university's most profound expansion evolved from a 1987 partnership that linked its medical school with several Pittsburgh hospitals. The University of Pittsburgh Medical Center, as it was named, soon became the largest health care system in southwestern Pennsylvania. Health sciences talent increased dramatically. Highly competitive National Institutes of Health research grants awarded to the university's researchers more than doubled in dollar value from 1992 to 2002, an indication the agency held the quality of the school's work and the expertise of those performing it in high regard.[13]

The turn toward leveraging the expertise of the region's research universities to rebalance the economy coincided for a time with administrations in Harrisburg that shared a similar view. "We were 'wave theorists,'" McNulty said of the administrations of Governor Tom Ridge and Governor Mark Schweiker, in which he served from 1995 to 2003 as policy director of the Department of Community and Economic Development and as its acting secretary. "We believed the viability of areas was determined by success in catching big waves of technology, and that we were in the middle of one—the beginning of the digital economy and the beginning of applying digital and computational capabilities to the life sciences." The viability of the Commonwealth, in their view, would be influenced by whether it could hitch a ride on one or more of those waves.

It was a moment when the state was willing to pursue its economic development vision with substantial funding, Donald F. Smith Jr. recalled. Smith, a Harvard University–trained economist with a doctorate in public policy from Carnegie Mellon University, was the executive director of the Carnegie Mellon Center for Economic Development in the late 1990s when he met with Jack Harding, the chief operating officer of the Silicon Valley computer software firm, Cadence Design Systems. Harding told Smith his company was desperate for talent, that he would "put a design center anywhere they could find 10 to 15 engineers. Smith continued: "He talked about opportunities of a seismic shift in the industry. I said, 'Jack, why aren't you in Pittsburgh?' He said I was asking the wrong question. 'You should be telling me why I should be in Pittsburgh.'" Smith returned to Carnegie Mellon and spoke with university and Pittsburgh Regional Alliance officials. A recruiting delegation dispatched to California met with Harding to pitch opportunities the region could offer a company such as his. The conversation turned to the idea of a public-private partnership that could bring the universities and industry together to innovate and speed the transfer of new technologies from the lab to the market. "Universities are fountains of knowledge and talent, but they have these big walls around them that are very hard to penetrate," Smith said. "Tech transfer and economic development was about creating portals into and out of the university."

Back in Pennsylvania, Smith, industry leaders, McNulty from the governor's office, and others drew up the concept for the Pittsburgh Digital Greenhouse and enlisted as partners three Pittsburgh universities, the Regional Alliance, the state and several companies, including Harding's Cadence Design Systems. The Greenhouse would offer technology companies a rare window into fertile university research labs, accelerate the development of new technologies—initially focused on the next generation of computer chips—and provide services that prepare entrepreneurs for the unforgiving realities of the business world they would face and capital to help promising companies get off the ground. "We ended up with about $30 million of state money for the effort," Smith recalled. "If you look at the robotics, autonomous and [artificial intelligence] companies here today, many of them, their founders or their faculty creators were funded by the Digital Greenhouse." Three years later, the Pittsburgh Life Science Greenhouse was created, receiving $100 million in state dollars to encourage commercialization of emerging technologies in the health sciences. "We hadn't done economic development initiatives of that scale in the region or in Pennsylvania in a very long time, maybe ever."

Universities also began to revisit their technology transfer policies, including how much of a cut they would take from companies born from the work of their faculty. Such policies could either assist or impede the creation of companies from university research, depending on how restrictive or expensive they were to entrepreneurs. Carnegie Mellon, which began restructuring its policies in the late 1990s, created a "five-percent-go-in-peace" program. The school eliminated the lengthy and complex process of trying to figure out what share of the company the university should receive for the contributions it made to the development of the idea that led to the start-up. Instead, the university would take a flat 5 percent, regardless of how the idea was developed. An additional point could be added for companies that are incubated on campus. The new approach had a profound effect. Once on opposite sides of the table, university officials and faculty researchers were now on the same side, working to move companies forward. Carnegie Mellon saw a nearly a tenfold increase in the number of start-up companies it spun out each year.

THE ECONOMIC LANDSCAPE SHIFTS

On August 1, 1988, controlled explosions reduced the Dorothy Six blast furnace at the former U.S. Steel Duquesne works to scrap. It ended a years-long campaign by labor activists to save it and demonstrated in a very public way that the age of steel dominance in southwestern Pennsylvania was over. Already, the heavy loss of manufacturing jobs and the rise of a more diverse economy was reshaping the southwestern Pennsylvania labor force and its demographics.

Remarkably, the labor force rebounded quickly. Not only had the number of workers increased beyond what it had been before the local steel industry collapsed, the regional labor force would reach its all-time peak in the late 1990s. Women were the reason why. The number of employed women grew by 42 percent from 1980 to 1998, while the number of employed men remained flat.[14] The population, however, continued to shrink, although the annual losses became smaller as the new century approached. At the same time, the number of residents who had earned a college degree soared. In 1980, only 14.5 percent of the population had a bachelor's degree or higher, which ranked as the 81st lowest rate among the 100 largest U.S. metro areas. Thirty years later, 40.5 percent of the population had a BA or higher, raising the region's rate to 23rd best in metro America.[15]

The regional job market also changed dramatically as the new century neared. Health care, higher education, finance, service, and tech industries were steadily adding jobs, while jobs in manufacturing continued to disappear. Hospitals and health care and the universities became the region's leading employers. The tech sector was a rising star. It was the kind of diversified economy that RIDC and its founders envisioned some 45 years earlier.

Economic recovery was uneven, however. The industrial suburbs, which had suffered the most during the crisis, continued to struggle. Nearly one dozen southwestern Pennsylvania cities and boroughs were subject to state intervention under a distressed municipalities act adopted to help stabilize their troubled economies in 1987. In the Mon Valley, Duquesne, East Pittsburgh, Clairton, Rankin, Braddock, North Braddock, and Homestead were on the list. The Beaver County steel towns of Aliquippa and Ambridge were included. The City of Pittsburgh would be added to the list in 2003. Others, such as McKeesport, barely escaped it. Reviving them was viewed as fraught with challenges. The authors of the Strategy 21 recovery plan found the notion of turning around the industrial Mon Valley intimidating. "Dependence on a single economic base—the metals industry—has jeopardized the economic survival of this region," they wrote. Their recommendations for investing in the revival of the Mon Valley were modest, including a metals retention/reuse study and small, mostly infrastructure improvement projects in a handful of communities.[16] RIDC's commitment was more substantial, but it came at the cost of acquiring large amounts of debt that strained its finances and tempered its ambitions. Keystone Commons, once the Westinghouse East Pittsburgh plant, had attracted enough small companies to cover its operating expenses by the end of the 20th century. The redeveloped U.S. Steelworks in McKeesport and Duquesne added tenants more slowly and continued to take losses until the reluctance of others to invest in those Mon Valley towns began to melt.

RIDC's industrial parks, both in the suburbs and the Mon Valley, reflected the new characteristics of the local economy, drawing tenants in health care, finance, light manufacturing, technology, and research. RIDC had become the developer of choice for expanding the research base of the region's major universities. The research facilities it helped finance and build filled quickly, lowering the financial risk to RIDC's involvement in such projects and providing some relief to its bottom line. All three of the University Technology Development Centers it built were fully leased by the end of the century, including one entirely occupied by Magee Women's Hospital as a research center.[17] "There are a lot of places that go through economic transitions where the earth doesn't move for a long time," McNulty observed. "RIDC got into East Pittsburgh, Duquesne and McKeesport and started to move earth. I don't think you can overestimate the psychological dynamics of that. If the earth doesn't start moving, there is no sense of momentum going forward. Before you can go with a tech strategy, people need to see earth moving and change happening."

The arrival of a new century would find four Pittsburgh foundations negotiating to buy the remaining acres of the former Jones & Laughlin steelworks in Pittsburgh's Hazelwood neighborhood. What had been reduced to an industrial brownfield with a few skeletal remnants of once-prosperous mills left standing had the potential to become the southern-most tip of the innovation corridor that was expanding through the nearby Carnegie Mellon and University of Pittsburgh campuses. RIDC would soon move more earth.

Mill 19

The Making of a New Pittsburgh Icon

The new century wasn't a year old when Frank Brooks Robinson confided to the RIDC board that four Pittsburgh foundations were going to make a bid to buy the undeveloped acreage of the former Jones & Laughlin Pittsburgh works and wanted the nonprofit to join them as one of the most experienced developers of industrial brownfields in the country.[1] He was interested. It was the last great brownfield within the City of Pittsburgh. It was an opportunity to turn a rusting specter of decline into a symbol of a prosperous future on 178 acres along the Monongahela River at a time when the city had begun to value its rivers and riverfronts as amenities rather than industrial workhorses. The Hazelwood neighborhood surrounding it, reeling from nearly two decades of neglect and disinvestment, was desperate for a reason to hope. The site was less than two miles from the University of Pittsburgh campus, three miles from Carnegie Mellon. Robinson saw the potential for another industrial park concentrating research institutions, technology companies, and talent that would complete the conversion of the city's once heavily industrialized Second Avenue corridor, where the Pittsburgh Technology Center was rising from the former Eliza Furnace portion of the J&L works with RIDC's help. The foundations, although they didn't have a specific plan in mind, leaned toward a similar idea, adding housing, recreation, and, perhaps, a curated mix of retail to turn industrial blight into a new community that would raise the prospects of the neighborhood at large.

The foundations were more certain of what they didn't want to see happen. The city, flirting with the notion of buying the former steel mill property itself, had discussed using it as a new location for its auto pound or enticing a metallurgical coke plant to take it over, despite the grow-ing list of abandoned steel mills up and down the river that underscored the long odds of it succeeding. Hearing such proposals compelled the foundation partners to act. "We felt that if that is what you start the project with, you're going in the wrong direction from the very begin-ning," recalled Maxwell King, who from 1999 to 2008 was president of the Heinz Endowments, one of the partners.

The partnership bought the former J&L Steel Hazelwood site from the bankrupt LTV Corporation for $10 million in 2002. The Almono partnership—the name cobbled from the names of the city's three rivers—included the Heinz Endowments, the Richard King Mellon Foundation, Claude Worthington Benedum Foundation, and McCune Foundation. RIDC was included as general partner. Years earlier, some RIDC board members had cautioned against becoming involved in the risky and expensive rehabilitation of shuttered steel mills in the Mon Valley, even suggesting the nonprofit sell those it had taken control of. By 2002, RIDC's debt had reached worrisome levels with much of it tied to those projects. But if there was strong opposition to the Hazelwood arrangement, it was not reported in the record. Robinson, in fact, told the board the Almono limited partnership structure would lessen the risk to RIDC, if the nonprofit chose to become involved. "I had the foun-dations behind me," he recalled. Their focus was on executing a quality development, the specifics of which were pending. They had patient money to invest. "They said they've got all the time in the world to see it done right. The signal given to me was, let's do it right. We're not in any hurry."

Sixteen years would pass before ground was broken to begin con-struction of the first building at the site. Robinson would retire as RIDC president, as would his successor, before the nonprofit reached the end of the long, winding road that led to its most acclaimed architectural accomplishment and new tenants who would burnish Pittsburgh's repu-tation as a national hub of technology innovation.

In the meantime, RIDC continued to rehabilitate other proper-ties that had been casualties of the region's economic decline. It would acquire another abandoned steelworks in the city and another in the suburbs. It bought the 80-year-old Pittsburgh home of the National Biscuit Company after the commercial bakery announced it was leaving town. It would briefly explore the housing market, developing apartments in a section of Downtown Pittsburgh that was being transformed from a seedy "red light" district to the city's Cultural District. And RIDC would again partner with Carnegie Mellon University and build a center on its campus that would bring the largest, most successful technology companies in America to Pittsburgh.

A COSTLY BAKERY RESCUE

The National Biscuit Company had made crackers in Pittsburgh for 80 years when it told state officials in Harrisburg it planned on moving out. State officials relayed the news to the city: the sturdy seven-story brick Nabisco plant in the city's East Liberty neighborhood, from which the smell of baking crackers had wafted since 1918, was scheduled to close. The news did not take the city by surprise. The company had tried to close the East Liberty operation in 1982 but dropped its plans when labor unions, churches, neighborhood groups, and others formed a coalition that threated a nationwide boycott of Nabisco products and pressured banks and city officials to work with the company to keep the plant open.[2] Once again, city officials met with the company, hoping to salvage the jobs of the 350 people still employed at the bakery that during its best years employed more than 1,000. The city had recently lost three steel mills, several corporate headquarters, and other businesses. Losing another employer could slow the incremental progress being made to revitalize Downtown and bring vibrancy and people to a financially unstable city.

But Nabisco's mind was made up this time around. The company had already begun consolidating production in newer, more modern factories, closing its older bakeries nationwide rather than invest in upgrading them. It would not make Pittsburgh an exception. The East Liberty bakery made its last batches of Ritz crackers, Wheat Thins, Better Cheddars, and Ritz Bits on November 19, 1998. The closing led city and Allegheny County officials to enlist the help of RIDC to save the building, the value of which was pointing up given its close proximity to

Carnegie Mellon and the University of Pittsburgh and the rising demand for real estate near their campuses.

Seven months later, an agreement was reached for RIDC to buy the 6.5-acre property—building and commercial baking equipment included—for $9.5 million. RIDC, cash-strapped at the time, borrowed the money, including a Pennsylvania Industrial Development Authority loan and a loan from the Strategic Investment Fund, which raised private-sector contributions to support local economic development projects. RIDC recruited another commercial bakery, the Atlantic Baking Group, to lease the building and retain the employees. The company, which soon changed its name to Bake-Line, made generic crackers over the next three years. Market conditions were difficult, however. Bake-Line filed for bankruptcy in 2004, having failed to get enough of its crackers on supermarket shelves to stay in business.

Lee Gevaudan, RIDC's director of development, recalled entering the bakery to assess its condition after the bankruptcy. "There was cracker dough still in large containers. There were lockers with clothing in it. They just stopped working and left." The plant was cleaned and rehabbed. But another tenant could not be found. RIDC was carrying $6.5 million of debt and had $1.4 million of cash equity invested in sparing the historic bakery from the wrecking ball and rehabbing it. With no rent coming in, it was a financial albatross. It was not the first time RIDC was left with debt on projects it undertook at the request of local government. Years earlier, RIDC bought the Clark Candy plant on the city's North Side at the request of the city, which was hoping to prevent the company from moving out. When the company was unable to avoid bankruptcy, RIDC was left with the debt and no rent payments coming in to pay it down, prompting Robinson to remark, "keeping Clark in Pittsburgh may have been good for the community, but it was not a good deal for RIDC."[3]

～

Frank Brooks Robinson retired from RIDC in 2003, ending a career that began when he was hired as a young architect 40 years earlier. As president, he guided the nonprofit through the region's most challenging economic era; convinced the board to approve risky acquisitions of shuttered steel mills and abandoned factories; oversaw the challenging redevelopment of each, as well as the expansion of the suburban parks; and built partnerships with the region's universities, which the nonprofit long recognized as engines of a new, more diversified economy. RIDC even broke from tradition to develop housing in Downtown Pittsburgh.

RIDC bought the Penn Garrison complex in the heart of the city's emerging Cultural District in 1990, having relocated the previous occupant—the homegrown nutritional products company GNC—to another part of the city to prevent it from moving out of state. The Pittsburgh Cultural Trust, under the leadership of its first president, Carol Brown, was engaged at that time in promoting the cultural and economic growth of Downtown Pittsburgh through the development of a fourteen-block arts and entertainment center in downtown Pittsburgh, which became known as the Cultural District. RIDC worked with the Cultural Trust to repurpose Penn Garrison from a worn office building into apartments. The Trust wanted to complement its conversion of several Downtown blocks where porn theaters, prostitution, and drug dealing were concentrated into a home for the arts, where decaying movie houses and theaters were being restored to splendor and new ones were being built. More residents, it was hoped, would attract and sustain more retail establishments and restaurants in a downtown that emptied out at the end of the workday. RIDC finished converting Penn Garrison into one of the first new Downtown apartment buildings in 2002 and managed the complex until it was sold nine years later, when more developers came to recognize value in underused buildings as apartments and condos. Downtown residency rose 55 percent from 2000 to 2020.[4]

Robert C. Stephenson was chosen to succeed Robinson as RIDC's president. He had been a seasoned real estate developer and broker for the DeBartolo Corporation and president of the Strategic Investment Fund, a pool of private capital established in 1996 with contributions from businesses, foundations, and individuals to be used to fill funding gaps in critical economic development projects throughout southwestern Pennsylvania.

From the start of his tenure, Stephenson was focused on improving RIDC's financial condition. He found the nonprofit's finances troubling, even with USX having agreed to forgive the $3.7 million RIDC owed it for the former McKeesport and Duquesne steel mill properties—a deal Robinson made before leaving office, reminding the steelmaker during negotiations how much money RIDC saved the company by undertaking the environmental remediation of the properties.

"RIDC has need to intensely focus on its finances and management," Stephenson told the board in his first annual review of the nonprofit's performance.[5] He favored raising rents when leases were renewed and aggressively collecting delinquent payments. "We are cracking the whip to make tenants pay up," he declared.[6] With his eye fixed on improving the bottom line, he was less inclined to take on projects that carried a financial risk and was willing to sell RIDC-owned properties that did.

One of the first to go was the former Nabisco bakery in East Liberty. Carrying heavy debt and not generating rental income, it was posting a loss every month. RIDC sold the 6.5-acre bakery property at a loss to a private developer for $5.25 million shortly after the building's only tenant filed for bankruptcy and moved out. The sale would get RIDC "out of a difficult financial situation," Stephenson said. He conceded "it would have been nice to redevelop the property." But given the shape of the nonprofit's finances, "RIDC needed to sell and move on."[7] Pittsburgh-based Walnut Capital would later redevelop it as a complex of retail, office, and housing and called it Bakery Square. Among the first tenants on the property were the retailers West Elm and Anthropologie. The most impactful was the tech giant Google, originally located in the Collaborative Innovation Center (CIC) built by RIDC on the Carnegie Mellon campus. As it outgrew that space, there were plans for it to relocate to the next CIC to be constructed, but it found a home instead in the renovated bakery, filling most of the space in that building.

Stephenson also negotiated an agreement to sell the former Edgewater Steelworks along the Allegheny River in the Borough of Oakmont, east of the City of Pittsburgh. RIDC acquired the 34-acre steelworks at the request of the Pennsylvania Industrial Development Authority following the company's first bankruptcy in 1997, intending to lease it back to the steelmaker with an option to buy. RIDC took full control after the steel-maker's third bankruptcy, razed the mill, sold the scrap to cover those costs, and completed the environmental remediation. But the nonprofit couldn't find a buyer interested in the property for industrial use. After sitting on the market for three years, its value as a riverside residential site was recognized by KACIN, a Westmoreland County development company. The developer bought the property for $4.5 million, in a deal that RIDC financed. RIDC netted $2.4 million once the property was paid off.[8] It would become Edgewater at Oakmont, a community of single-family houses, apartments, and townhouses set against a nicely landscaped riverfront, where four-bedroom homes sold for as much as $2.4 million or more in 2024.

When he wasn't focusing on balancing the books, Stephenson concentrated on administrative changes he believed were necessary. He felt the nonprofit was still poorly understood and hired a part-time communications consultant to improve its "image/identity, as well as inform folks and organizations of its activities and special abilities in economic development." In particular, he wanted the public to understand RIDC is "different than virtually all economic development agencies," in that, even as a nonprofit, it pays taxes. RIDC was paying more than $4 million a year in real estate taxes on its properties, and it had paid more than $51 million in real estate taxes to local governments and school districts over its first 50 years. Stephenson also directed RIDC to begin to draft a strategic plan before he left office, telling the board, "In practice, RIDC has, for a good number of years, managed to function . . . without a real 'game plan' for business maintenance, growth and financial stability."[9]

Stephenson retired at the end of 2008. In the 46 years that had passed since RIDC stepped into the role of commercial developer, it had accumulated a portfolio of 59 buildings with nearly 5.4 million square feet of office, research, and light industrial space. Progress toward stabilizing the nonprofit's financial health was on track, he told the board, citing rent increases, collection of delinquent accounts, the weeding out of "bad tenants," and the sale of properties as reasons for the improvement.[10, 11] RIDC was now "practicing sound operating and budgeting practices," which he believed would help it navigate rough waters ahead, as the Great Recession, which began a year earlier, deepened.

INFLECTION POINT

Donald Smith Jr. had just taken the position of vice president of economic development for both Carnegie Mellon and the University of Pittsburgh when he was invited to join the RIDC board in 2003. He had run Carnegie Mellon's Center for Economic Development, an applied research center, representing the school in several initiatives aimed at leveraging the expertise of the region's research universities as an economic driver, including the creation of the Digital Greenhouse and Life Sciences Greenhouse. He knew of RIDC's work. His contact with the nonprofit included representing Carnegie Mellon on the community advisory board established by the Almono partners—RIDC being one —to solicit input on the redevelopment of the former J&L steelworks in Hazelwood. His impression of RIDC before he took a seat on its board, he recalled, "wasn't super positive and wasn't negative, either. It was, they were there. They were another economic development organization. I appreciated the industrial parks but didn't necessarily connect them to what I was doing at the universities so much. The Software Engineering Institute [built by RIDC] was great, but it wasn't that commercially focused." He hadn't considered real estate to be much of a factor in fostering the growth of a technology sector. "I'd always been, eh, real estate—buildings are buildings. It's more about talent and venture capital and that stuff."

RIDC had already begun to arrange low-interest state economic development loans and some commercial loans to build a four-story Collaborative Innovation Center on the campus of Carnegie Mellon when Smith attended his first board meeting. The center, perched atop a hollow at the edge of campus, was designed to allow for rapid reconfiguration of open landscape workspace to encourage collaboration. It was built to high green-building standards, earning Leadership in Energy and Environmental Design Gold designation. Its purpose was to provide laboratory and office space to companies that wanted to collaborate with Carnegie Mellon on innovative projects, giving them access to the wealth of research, and faculty and student talent, the school had to offer. It was an immediate hit.

The Collaborative Innovation Center drew some of the nation's leading technology companies to Pittsburgh soon after it opened in 2005. Apple was an early tenant. Intel, one of the world's largest manufacturers of semiconductor chips, moved in. Disney installed its research studios there. One year after it opened, the center welcomed Google, the most significant technology company of the time.

Google had set out to create centers of engineering excellence in locations other than northern California's Silicon Valley. The key factor in deciding where to put them was the expertise the company could tap into. In Pittsburgh, Google found the intellectual capability and sense of entrepreneurship it sought in Andrew Moore, a Carnegie Mellon computer science professor, entrepreneur, and leading expert in machine learning. In addition, the Collaborative Innovation Center offered an incentive other locations couldn't. "Google was intrigued with the notion that you could be within walking distance of the No. 1 computer science school in the country," recalled Timothy McNulty, who had recently returned to Carnegie Mellon as associate provost and special assistant to the provost after eight years in Harrisburg serving in the administrations of two Pennsylvania governors.

Google Pittsburgh started with two people. Five years later, with 100 employees and plans to expand further, it moved into the former Nabisco plant in Bakery Square, where its payroll swelled to more than 800. "There is no question that Google was a massive inflection point for us becoming a much more established tech center, and there is absolutely no question that the Collaborative Innovation Center was pivotal," McNulty said. "It became a physical validation that the university can incubate things and they can get big. There is no Bakery Square without Google and no Google [Pittsburgh] without the Collaborative Innovation Center." Apple, another Silicon Valley company, followed a different path to Pittsburgh. After resigning from the company in 1985, co-founder Steve Jobs spent several months in Pittsburgh when he was working on new projects, including the NeXT computer workstation and a software company. Jobs returned to Apple more than a decade later. With Jobs at the helm, Apple acquired a small start-up company founded by Carnegie Mellon graduate students whom he had discovered during his time in the city. The acquisition led Apple to open a satellite research lab in Pittsburgh in 2005 and eventually locate with a much larger presence in the Assembly building in the city's Bloomfield neighborhood. Although Apple and Google took different routes to Pittsburgh, they were drawn to the same talent, campus, and opportunities the Collaborative Innovation Center offered.

It was not lost on Smith. "I had done a lot of tech-based economic development work and research throughout my career. The ability to get Google, Apple, Intel and Disney to open [research and development] centers in Pittsburgh because of the real estate and proximity to the university talent base was eye-opening. The value of real estate became apparent to me." Smith would have the opportunity to apply the lesson elsewhere in the coming years. He became the sixth president of RIDC in 2009, following Stephenson's retirement. With it came the challenge of redeveloping the largest industrial brownfield left in the City of Pittsburgh that had stalled in the seven years after four foundations bought it with visions of remaking it as another symbol of the region's rebirth.

Arrested Development

The Reverend Leslie Boone would watch the tumbleweed dance across the brownfield that had been the J&L steelworks from her office in the Hazelwood Presbyterian Church across the street. Most of the mills and shops that at one time employed Reverend Boone's grandfather and as many as 5,000 others had been razed by 2012. The property had been graded flat, like an open prairie. The tumbleweed, it seemed to her, was the only occupant. "Every time I looked, there would be nothing there but that tumbleweed. He'd just be rolling across that big empty space."[12]

Almono LP had bought the 178 industrial acres 10 years earlier with ambitions of remaking it as a model 21st-century community and possible tech hub. "Everybody was enthusiastic about it," recalled King, the former president of the Heinz Endowments. "Then, like the dog that catches the car, we had to figure out what we wanted to do with it."

The four foundations in the partnership had no development experience. They had a general vision for the site, but nothing specific or firm. "We all agreed that Pittsburgh would really benefit from a New Urbanist community that included academia, residential, commercial. And that it would be another example of the foundations helping Pittsburgh use its riverfronts effectively." The foundations hired architectural planning firms to help them think through the options. The results were "all pie-in-the-sky," he said. RIDC was invited into the partnership as general partner because of its development experience, particularly with steel mill brownfields, and its successes in securing state development funding for redevelopment.

RIDC was unfamiliar with the dynamics of such a partnership, with limited partners expecting to have direct input into development decisions. The foundations drafted a set of principles to guide development in line with their aspirations for the built environment, and the economic and social impact of the project. Several master plans were commissioned and revised, then others were commissioned to replace them over the course of nearly two decades. Adapting to such a process was a challenge for RIDC at times. The most difficult was convincing the partners to allow for the construction of at least one building. In RIDC's view, the sooner buildings appear on a site, the sooner a market is established, investors get interested, and prospective tenants come to see it as a place to move to. The approach had worked at its suburban business parks and was adopted at its other brownfield reclamation projects. Smith believed a building or buildings at the Hazelwood brownfield would be a "pump-primer."

The barren site wasn't attracting much interest. The partners could not find a suitable for-profit developer who shared their vision, embraced the site guidelines, and was willing to invest money in the project as well. "We've been very consistent in resisting the one-off proposed uses of the property and wanting to develop it according to a plan," said William Getty, president of the Benedum Foundation, in a 2012 interview. "When we got into this, the expectation was that there was an advantage to having patient investors controlling the last large piece of developable riverfront property in the city, although I don't think we ever dreamed that patience would mean more than 10 years."[13] Even more patience would be necessary.

Redevelopment of Hazelwood Green, which the partnership named the brownfield site, faced several complications during the long period of inactivity on the ground. One was the lingering uncertainty over the route of the northern section of the Mon-Fayette Expressway, conceived in the 1950s as a high-speed highway connecting Morgantown, West Virginia, and Pittsburgh. Pennsylvania Turnpike Commission planners had the 10-mile northern spur knifing through the Hazelwood Green property at one point, bedeviling designers of the brownfield redevelopment master plan, rendering more than 35 acres useless, restricting options for reusing the site, and diminishing its overall value. For a time, designers took to drawing up two versions of the master plan—one without the expressway dividing the site and one dealing with the expressway in various ways, including the idea of installing 750-foot-wide lids over the expressway that could be used for anything from parking lots to athletic fields while serving as a bridge to the Hazelwood neighborhood. But cash-strapped state budgets and other factors led the state to suspend construction of the expressway spur. [14] When it later returned to the construction schedule, the route had been altered and the new plans avoided disrupting the Hazelwood Green development.

The Great Recession, which lasted from late 2007 into 2009, was another complication. The climate of tight money and risk aversion that followed led to a reassessment of whether there was sufficient interest among private developers in the project as defined by the partnership and site guidelines. The answer up until then was, no. "If we are going to wait for a developer with deep pockets and miles-long vision to come, take over and agree to do the shared Almono vision with the developer's dollars, we're going to be sitting here when my grandchildren are working for a living," Smith warned them.

RIDC had learned to expect unforeseen complications and delays at brownfield sites once a shovel was put into the ground. Hazelwood Green was no exception. Timothy White, who joined RIDC as assistant vice president of development in 2011, had a personal connection to the steel industry and the former J&L steelworks. His grandfather worked at Mill 19 for 25 years before suffering a heart attack, which ended his working days. "I would always hear about the mill. That was my first introduction—that and in elementary school we had to learn the Bessemer process," he said, referring to the steelmaking process that revolutionized the industry more than a century earlier. White's first meeting on the Hazelwood Green project involved negotiating with two railroads for public access underneath a rail overpass. It took 10 years to resolve.

RIDC convinced the Almono partnership to install water and sewage lines, roads and intersections, utility trunk lines, and other basic infrastructure to make Hazelwood Green more attractive to private developers. More complications arose. Tons of buried concrete and steel that had served as the foundations for the mills and furnaces were discovered, which crews were unable to remove. More than 800,000 cubic yards of fill was brought in to cap environmental issues. Four to 12 feet of cover were needed to satisfy a state remediation plan and to raise several areas above the flood plain. The fill, obtained at no cost, was taken from the development of the South Side Works retail and housing project across the river and construction of a rapid-transit tunnel under the Allegheny River linking Downtown Pittsburgh to the North Shore with its football stadium, major league baseball park, and other entertainment venues. Negotiations to resolve issues in securing a long list of required permits also slowed development. The Almono partners expected to address stormwater and sewage by building new lines to serve the site. The Pittsburgh Water and Sewage Authority, however, wanted the partners to replace or repair the existing storm lines, which were aged and in disrepair. It took longer than a year to reach a settlement that would have RIDC replace one line, repair another, and abandon the rest. A long debate over whether to allow stormwater in retention ponds to filter into the groundwater would involve the highest ranks of the state Department of Environmental Protection before the question was resolved. It took longer than one year and the involvement of the governor's office in Harrisburg for the Pennsylvania Historical Museum Commission to withdraw its demand that the remediated brownfield be excavated for historical artifacts, in addition to two already developed sites the Almono partners did not own. The city required RIDC to do a 20-year traffic study on the full development of the site, a challenge given the overall vision and plan was still in flux. Development waited as RIDC worked with city officials to avoid having to build a traffic circle at the east end of Hazelwood Green that would make it difficult for large trucks to navigate the site. And because part of the site touched a state road, a state highway occupancy permit was added to the list of permits the Almono partners had to secure for development to proceed.

The foundations made an additional investment to finance preparation costs. Financing the overall development became less tenuous when Almono LP received the largest tax increment financing package in the city's history. Tax increment financing allows for capturing the future tax benefits of improvements made on the property and using the money to pay present-day costs of making the improvements.[15]

RIDC tried to persuade the Almono partners to give it operational control of the site and begin construction of several buildings. The nonprofit recruited local developers to do the work. "We talked about printing T-shirts to hand out that said, 'Vertical in 2014,'" Smith recalled. "The concern among partners was: 'How do we know you're going to do the vision we want?' We had the [latest] master plan and said we were committed to that plan. But we couldn't get the partners to approve moving forward to do the first wave of development." As it turned out, the vision among the foundation partners of what the site could become was still evolving, as was the leadership at the foundations. The partners increasingly saw in Hazelwood Green the opportunity to create a national model of sustainable development. At the same time, the foundations were concerned about the impact Hazelwood Green would have on the Hazelwood neighborhood and were exploring ways to strengthen the neighborhood to put residents in position to benefit from the development, rather than be displaced by it.

The "Choicest" Neighborhood

Hazelwood was once the place to be in the City of Pittsburgh. Named for the hazelnut trees along the banks of the Monongahela River, it was once described by a city newspaper as "the choicest suburban section" in

19th-century Pittsburgh for its fine homes, splendid lawns, and unobstructed view of the river and forested valley below.[16] Stephen Foster spent time there as a guest of a prominent resident, writing some of his classic American folk songs on the piano in the parlor. Then came the Industrial Revolution. For nearly 100 years, Hazelwood was part of one of the region's largest steelworks. Its sprawling complex of bar, billet, and cold-finishing mills, furnaces, and coke ovens brought unprecedented growth and prosperity to the neighborhood. It also blanketed the neighborhood with the sulfurous odor of heavy pollution, leaving it unfit to hold the title of the city's "choicest" place to live. After the steelworks closed and the heavy smoke lifted, the once-bustling neighborhood became a specter of post-industrial decline, enduring years of disinvestment and isolation.

When its mills were humming, nearly 5,000 people were employed at the steelworks before Jones & Laughlin Steel sold it to LTV in 1974. In 1960, nearly 12,800 people and 200 businesses called Hazelwood home.[17] The population thinned to only 4,300 residents in 2010, more than a decade after the steelworks closed. The incomes of 24 percent of its residents fell below the federal poverty line. Thirteen percent of residents did not have a high school diploma or equivalent, nearly twice the citywide average. More than half of the houses were 100 years old or older. Some 27 percent of properties were vacant, including 19 percent of the housing. Sixty-two percent of the houses sold in 2010 were bought for $10,000 or less.[18] Businesses had dwindled to a handful. The neighborhood's public middle school and elementary school were closed for lack of students. Churches were closed for lack of parishioners, including Reverend Boone's Hazelwood Presbyterian Church. Bus routes were eliminated for lack of riders, although more than a quarter of workers still living in the neighborhood relied on Port Authority of Allegheny County buses to get to work.

Residents who remained in the neighborhood were skeptical when the Almono partners bought the former steelworks and announced intentions to redevelop it in a way that could point the neighborhood toward a brighter future. Hazelwood had been the subject of upwards of a dozen analyses, studies, and blueprints for revival following the closing of the mill, none of which led to meaningful improvements in the neighborhood or the quality of life of those who lived there. Residents did, however, have strong opinions about what they wanted to see happen on the site. "Many in Hazelwood, but not all, felt it was time for something new—that, because of the high level of pollution from those plants and the growth of the high-tech industry, steel's time had come and gone," Jim Richter observed in 2012, when he was the director of the Hazelwood Initiative, the neighborhood's community development corporation.[19]

They were also firm about what they didn't want. "Not like the Waterfront," was a common refrain, referring to the 1.2 million-square-foot, privately developed shopping and entertainment complex that replaced the U.S. Steel Homestead works in nearby Homestead and West Homestead boroughs. Located along the river, its design allowed patrons to come and go without leaving its sprawling parking lot or road grid. Despite its large size and popularity, the shopping complex was seen as doing little to improve the conditions in the boroughs, which like other post-industrial steel towns in the Mon Valley were grave. In Hazelwood, there was a sense that their Homestead neighbors had been shortchanged. Hazelwood residents didn't want the Almono-owned brownfield in their neighborhood to be redeveloped as an "island that people visit and leave and ignore the fact there's a community here."[20]

Investment began to find Hazelwood, mostly in philanthropic dollars. Even after more than a decade of lying barren, the neighborhood's brownfield had the aura of great potential.

MILL 19

One of the last steelmaking structures left standing from the former Jones & Laughlin Pittsburgh works was Mill 19. It was built during World War II to bolster wartime production, was put to work turning out 10-inch bar steel as a rolling mill during peacetime, and used as a place to store coke oven brick during its final days as part of LTV Steel, when the company was staggering into bankruptcy. In 2014, it was a four-football-fields-long empty shell, a place where pigeons roosted. RIDC saw it as an opportunity to bring the brownfield its first new building. The building itself was imagined as new construction abiding to sustainable design standards built within the steel skeleton of the original mill. It would anchor an "eco-tech" district on the site, a campus linked to nearby universities with space for early-stage university spin-outs as well as corporate-sponsored research, that could become a "Silicon Valley landing zone" for transplanted companies and a magnet for top talent in emerging technologies.[21]

RIDC reached a tentative agreement with the Almono partners early the following year to trade its interests as general partner for Mill 19 and some additional land. The agreement would allow the nonprofit to begin redeveloping Mill 19 as what Smith described as a "fast-moving project."[22] It did not move as quickly as hoped. RIDC was in uncharted waters when it came to the partnership's decision-making process. It was asked to oversee development, but did not have site control. Approval of projects required a consensus among the partners. A design review committee—something RIDC had never dealt with before—was established to ensure the quality of what is built meets the aspirations of the partnership. Dozens of public meetings were held with Hazelwood residents to listen to their desires for the development. An ambitious set of principles guiding development reflected the foundations' desire to demonstrate the highest vision of what America's discarded brownfields could become. As RIDC understood them, the economic and social principles included making Hazelwood Green a place that would stimulate the growth of quality jobs and local investment, preserve the diversity of the neighborhood, serve existing residents, and attract new ones. It was to provide public access to the river and unfold in ways that would complement the existing neighborhood and enable the community to share the benefits of the development. Urban design principles and best practices would apply across the site. Buildings were required to be of high quality. Advanced sustainability practices would apply. Creative design and development were encouraged.[23] Energy efficiency and other sustainability practices were particularly important to the partners. The Heinz Endowments was heavily invested. It had, for example, provided seed money to establish the Pittsburgh Green Building Alliance, a nonprofit that promotes energy efficiency in the commercial building sector, and it had organized a series of annual conferences that brought global leaders in sustainability to Pittsburgh to share their experiences and introduce new concepts.

RIDC's Mill 19 (above) was once part of a sprawling Jones & Laughlin steel production operation. After more than 100 years of production and a merger in 1984 to form LTV Steel, the factories remained in use into the 1990s and finally closed for good in 1997. Credit: Rivers of Steel

Most of the buildings on the site were demolished and the property remediated, while Mill 19 remained (bottom left and top right), empty and rusting but with its strong steel superstructure still intact. Its innovative redesign and revitalization after RIDC took ownership includes nearly 300,000 square feet of new buildings constructed within the original steel structure, and environmental features including the largest sloped rooftop solar array in the country (bottom right, credit: Corey Gaffer Photography).

The success of this project has served as a beacon for the region and a symbol of Pittsburgh's revitalization. It regularly receives prominent visitors, including President Biden, members of the president's cabinet, and government officials and groups from around the world.

From the beginning, balancing pace-setting aspirations against the economic realities of commercial development was a challenge and a source of tension. At issue was controlling the cost of development to allow for leasing space on the site at rates affordable to the tenants the partners hoped to attract. The partnership process itself had its own learning curve. "I'm still working with the partners to achieve clarity of operating procedures," Smith told the RIDC board after proposing to redevelop Mill 19. A few months after RIDC received approval to move forward on Mill 19, the project was put on hold. "We have not yet been able to reach accommodation with the partners on the site control needed for bank financing, and to warrant additional investment in project design," Smith reported, adding that there was "some concern about RIDC playing both the land developer and vertical developer roles on site."[24]

The partners commissioned another master plan. When it failed to win approval of all of the partners, RIDC officials began to reconsider the nonprofit's role in Hazelwood Green. There was concern among some of the partners "that if we do the first building and we don't do it in an 'intergalactically green' manner, we can only go down from there. We can't go up," Smith recalled. "To me, that is the opposite of how the development business works. The development business is, you build the best you can build today. Once you build some demand, you build the market. You can increase the standards over time because you've increased the attractiveness, you've demonstrated the market, you've got the momentum. Development is a momentum game." RIDC still believed in the site's potential to further spur the development of the region as a technology hub. But, Smith said, "we can't be responsible for this development without having authority to execute."

When RIDC had proposed exchanging its share in the Almono partnership for Mill 19 and another 5.5 acres alongside it, "part of the rationale was we didn't have operational control so we couldn't be in charge," Smith recalled. "And part of it was, 'Look, nobody else is going to come and build a spec project here under these terms. We're just crazy enough to do that because that's our role.'" The arrangement was made final in October 2016. Within two months, Carnegie Mellon signed up to occupy a large portion of the not-yet-built Mill 19. The university was competing for the federal government's Advanced Robotics for Manufacturing Institute and wanted its pitch to include Mill 19 as its home. The institute was established to strengthen U.S. manufacturing by introducing innovations in advanced manufacturing technology, particularly robotics and artificial intelligence, and training a workforce capable of working with those technologies.

The university was awarded the institute the following year. Hazelwood Green had an anchor tenant. "The federal government was looking for this institute to be a bridge between the tech economy and the manufacturing economy," recalled McNulty, who was associate vice president for government relations at Carnegie Mellon when the school was competing for the institute. "Mill 19 was emblematic of what [the institute] was going to do. I'm not saying we might not have won [the institute] without Mill 19, but there is no question in my mind that it contributed a great deal to our success."

MSR Design, a Minneapolis-based architectural firm, was brought in to take the lead in designing Mill 19. MSR came up with the idea of keeping the original mill exoskeleton, use it as a solar shed and build new buildings within it. Solar panels installed atop the quarter-mile roof became the largest sloped rooftop solar array in the United States when Mill 19 opened in 2019. The electricity it generates provides power for two of the three buildings that are part of Mill 19. The envelope provides thermal efficiency and up to 96 percent daylight autonomy, a measure of how much of the time the building's lighting needs are met by daylight. Stormwater is managed with rain gardens and infiltration basins to give the city's overburdened stormwater and sewage system some relief. Rooftop rainwater is recycled for flushing restroom toilets. Outside, a landscaped "ruin" garden was made as a contemplative space that combines the remnants of old machinery foundations. The American Institute of Architects described Mill 19 as "a bold transformation of a former steel mill that now welcomes the sustainable future of advanced manufacturing"[25] when it awarded the building its 2023 COTE Top Ten Award for sustainable design, one of several national awards Mill 19 would earn.

More important to the region's economic trajectory were the tenants Mill 19 managed to attract. Joining the Advanced Robotics for Manufacturing Institute was another Carnegie Mellon project, the Manufacturing Futures Initiative, which creates new technologies that the institute then introduces to industry. Filling out Mill 19's first building were Catalyst Connection, a manufacturing industry nonprofit, and YKK AP, a Japan-based company in the building technology field. RIDC followed with another building built under the long solar canopy, anticipating that having Carnegie Mellon as an anchor tenant would attract companies engaged in related technologies that want to be near a center of innovation. The entire second mill building was leased by Motional. The Boston-based autonomous vehicle company, formed as a joint venture between Korean automaker Hyundai and Aptiv, a Dublin, Ireland-based maker of vehicle electronics, would bring 300 jobs to Pittsburgh. RIDC would open a third mill building in 2023.[26]

"I think we've ended up in a pretty good place," Smith said, reflecting on RIDC's experience at Hazelwood Green. "But I think had [the Almono partners] reached agreement to let us go forward with that plan in 2014, we'd have 1.5 million square feet on site now. But that's easy for me to say. This was a massive investment of foundation dollars. It's their site, their money and they have the right to set the standards they want. Our job was to advise them on what is economically feasible and we had differences of opinion with some of the external consultants who were brought in. Maybe it was just a process that had to play out to show what you could or couldn't do in order to get everyone on the same page. This was novel. It was visionary. And it is a big site, a heavy lift."

Grant Oliphant, as president of the Heinz Endowments from 2014 to 2022, was among the partners who most scrutinized the sustainability aspects of the site. "Don Smith probably considers me a terrible irritant. But I think we were good for each other," he said in an interview five years after Mill 19 opened. "You look at the building they ended up developing on Hazelwood Green. It's an extraordinary accomplishment and symbol. Nothing like what they would've built in their early days, or middle days. I think that was because they were being pushed to do great things and they ended up doing it. There is a history [in Pittsburgh] of disparate parties coming together to figure things out over time and good things happening as a result."

Beyond RIDC's slice of the Hazelwood Green site, a former railroad roundhouse had been renovated that once served the steelworks, but little else was happening on the more than 160 remaining acres. The Almono partners' search for a private developer to take on the acreage was slowed by a Pittsburgh market that tended to be more risk-averse than other cities steeped in technology innovation, such as Boston. "No matter how much infrastructure we were taking care of, from roads to sewage to the environmental remediation, the market in Pittsburgh—still, after all of these years—was not ready to support a for-profit coming in and taking on the risk and developing it on their own," recalled Sam Reiman, director of the Richard King Mellon Foundation, an Almono partner. "I sometimes joke that I spend my days solving a problem that doesn't exist in Boston. You can't account for the lack of market forces here. Even with the additional capital, it doesn't remedy the problem the way that one would hope." The foundation awarded the University of Pittsburgh a $100 million grant to launch its BioForge, a partnership with biotech company ElevateBio, to accelerate the development of cell and gene therapies. It was the largest single grant awarded by the foundation in its 75-year history. The grant included a provision that the BioForge be built at Hazelwood Green. The foundation included a similar provision when it awarded a grant for Carnegie Mellon's Robotics Innovation Center, which would feature wet lab, testing and development space, and a 50,000-square-foot drone cage.

Hazelwood Green began to draw investment toward the neighborhood itself. The nonprofit community development corporation, the Hazelwood Initiative, formed a limited partnership to buy the neighborhood's middle school, which had been vacant for longer than a decade after the Pittsburgh Public Schools closed it. The money came from the city Urban Redevelopment Authority and bank loans, which for a generation or so had been hard to come by in the neighborhood. Part of the school was converted to affordable housing as a hedge against an expected rise in speculation and property values and the threat of widespread displacement in Hazelwood, where half of the housing is rental. The remaining space would house a gym, theater and recording studio for arts programming, child care, a full-service health clinic, and small business incubator.

Foundations began investing heavily in the neighborhood, usually through community groups. The Heinz Endowments chose Hazelwood as the first neighborhood where it introduced a "place-based" strategy of focusing all of its grantmaking programs on a defined geographic area and working with residents to improve conditions. The Carnegie Library Hazelwood branch was rescued from closing and reopened in Reverend Boone's abandoned Hazelwood Presbyterian Church, which was renovated as an energy-efficient green building with child care and other family services offered on other floors. The neighborhood's shuttered elementary school was bought and reopened as a charter school. The business district started a slow comeback, adding a food market, a nonprofit catering service, and culinary arts training center and a popular French bakery. The 18th-century house where Stephen Foster once composed was resurrected as a Scottish pub. Twenty years after the Almono partners bought the former J&L steelworks, they found a private developer to build out the rest of the Hazelwood Green vision, signing an agreement with Tishman Speyer, an international developer whose projects included a Harvard University research campus in Boston, the redevelopment of Rockefeller Center in New York City, and the Chang'An steelworks in Beijing, which became one of the sites to host events during the 2022 Winter Olympics.[27]

Opportunity had come to Hazelwood, just as it had years earlier in the City of Pittsburgh Lawrenceville neighborhood, when a technology hub rose from unwanted industrial acreage along the Allegheny River and turned the tired manufacturing neighborhood into one of the hottest markets in the city.

Robotics Row

Lawrenceville approached the 21st century as a tired working-class neighborhood of the City of Pittsburgh with a single asset that would give rise to a cluster of robotics research, talent, and companies with transformative potential the rest of the technology world could not ignore. Its 1,350 acres are bordered by the Allegheny River to the north and lie three miles from Downtown. Before it became a city neighborhood, William Foster, father of American folk song composer Stephen Collins Foster, established it as a borough in 1834. Rather than name the place "Fosterville," after himself—a common practice at the time, which he considered—Foster decided to honor a fallen hero of the War of 1812, James Lawrence, captain of an ill-fated frigate, whose dying words, "Don't give up the ship!" endured as the mantra of the U.S. Navy well beyond the memory of his deeds. The neighborhood's sprawling arsenal was a critical munitions hub supplying the Union Army during the American Civil War. Andrew Carnegie entered the metals industry in Lawrenceville, building two ironworks there before building a steelmaking empire in the Mon Valley.[1] The entertainer Liberace remembered Lawrenceville as the place where St. Francis Hospital nurses—and God—saved him from a near-fatal reaction to chemicals used to clean his glittery wardrobe while he was performing in town in 1963.[2] When manufacturing collapsed in the region during the 1980s, Lawrenceville was among the first blue-collar enclaves to experience the consequences. Property values fell and young adults fled, leaving the neighborhood with one of the oldest populations in Pittsburgh as the factories, warehouses, and mills that crowded a narrow strip of bottom land along the river began to close. It was there, on the site of an abandoned foundry, that Carnegie Mellon University decided to build its National Robotics Engineering Center.

RIDC acquired a former Heppenstall Steel building and Geoffrey Boehm chocolate factory in Lawrenceville in 2002, at a time when Pittsburgh Magazine called the neighborhood "more down and out than up and coming." It transformed the site into the Lawrenceville Technology Center, which includes (top left) the "Blue Building," occupied by Carnegie Robotics, (middle left) the Chocolate Factory, a multi-tenant facility housing tech and life sciences companies, and (bottom left) Tech Forge, a new tech-flex building that is home to Caterpillar's autonomous technology group, Evoqua Water Technologies, and Innovation Works' Robotics Startup Factory. Credit: Photo by Elliot Cramer, Courtesy of Desmond Architects

Discussions between Carnegie Mellon and the National Aeronautics and Space Administration on a new model for robotics research began in 1994. Those involved included Red Whitaker, a Carnegie Mellon scientist and robotics pioneer, whose robots had demonstrated the field's commercial potential 15 years earlier by helping clean up the Three Mile Island nuclear power plant following its high-profile meltdown. Carnegie Mellon was one of the few universities to offer advanced education in robotics. Its resume included the Robotics Institute, the first robotics department established at a U.S. university. The university was the first to offer a Ph.D. in robotics. And it was attracting the brightest minds in the emerging field.

The National Robotics Engineering Center opened in 1996 on property assembled by RIDC with seed funding from the federal space agency. Its intent was to commercialize the ideas of the university's growing number of roboticists. The building itself was designed with their needs in mind, offering high bays and plenty of space to develop, tinker with, and test their ideas. There was enough room for large machines. Adjacent land offered outdoor testing space for projects that needed it, such as autonomous vehicles. The university's young roboticists were so eager to begin working there that many of them moved into trailers on the site while demolition and renovation of the former foundry was still being done.[3] The center would never employ more than 200 people, but its alumni would have an impact on the region's innovation economy.

One industry sector their expertise would give rise to was mobile autonomous systems. While self-driving cars and trucks are the most-mentioned examples of mobile autonomous technologies, their application is widely spread among industries that require smart, mobile equipment, including warehousing, manufacturing, mining, agriculture, and construction. Autonomous systems require numerous, distinct technologies to seamlessly work together. The complex technology "stack"— a software engineering term for the complete set of platforms and enabling components that create a fully functioning system—includes fundamental technologies, such as sensors that enable a system to perceive, interact, and communicate with the world around it; enabling technologies, such as machine learning and data fusion, which enable systems to make intelligent decisions from the information they gather; and other technologies that allow machines to manage specific tasks.[4] The National Robotics Engineering Center was at the forefront of the development of such technologies. Nearly two thirds of its alumni would remain in Pittsburgh. They would create some of the most promising robotics and autonomous systems companies in the nation. By 2020, at least three of five people employed by such companies could trace their roots to the center.[5]

~

RIDC's involvement in Lawrenceville's emergence as a technology hub began as a rescue mission one year before the National Robotics Engineering Center opened its doors. Geoffrey Boehm Chocolates, a local family-owned candymaker established in 1914, approached RIDC for help as it tried to stabilize its finances. The company had experienced a steep decline in sales of its chocolate, but expected business to pick up. It asked RIDC to buy its factory, a former warehouse for the Atlantic and Pacific Company's A&P grocery store chain built in 1930. The company preferred to lease the factory from RIDC, rather than own it. RIDC secured a low-interest loan from the Pennsylvania Industrial Development Authority, borrowed more money from a local bank, and bought the factory in 1995.[6]

The RIDC board was concerned about acquiring more debt at a time when it was borrowing heavily to finance the redevelopment of shuttered steel mills in the Mon Valley and the former Westinghouse Electric plant in East Pittsburgh. In selling the idea of buying the Geoffrey Boehm factory, RIDC president Frank Brooks Robinson told them a review of the company's finances found the chocolatier to be profitable, despite the recent setback. In addition, it had signed a new deal with a national fundraising organization, which was expected to boost future sales. Preserving the jobs at the Geoffrey Boehm plant was a priority. RIDC would be responsible for the loans, should the company fail. Even if that occurred, Robinson noted, RIDC would own a valuable property in Lawrenceville. The factory was just across 41st Street from the abandoned foundry where the National Robotics Engineering Center was being built.[7]

DOUBLING DOWN IN LAWRENCEVILLE

The Geoffrey Boehm factory was empty seven years later. The company had defaulted on its lease and loan[8] and moved production elsewhere. It managed to stay in business, however, and continued to sell its chocolates nationwide after rebranding, including from a retail store inside the Pentagon in Washington, D.C., likely the most secure candy store in the country. Robinson was winding down his career at RIDC in 2002 when he convinced the board to approve redeveloping the factory into a multiple-occupancy building for technology entrepreneurs, and to borrow more state PIDA loans and commercial loans to pay for it. The same year, he proposed buying another industrial building in Lawrenceville, the vacant Heppenstall steelworks, which sat on 14 acres adjacent to the National Robotics Engineering Center. The small steelmaker, known for its knives and razor blades, was among the first to close during the steel crisis. Its workers were laid off and its assets were sold in 1979, nearly 90 years after it opened. The mill, empty for more than two decades, had rusted into blight. It was an opportunity to add to the urban technology park Robinson envisioned rising around National Robotics Engineering Center.

He brought in Charles Thorpe, the director of the Robotics Institute on Carnegie Mellon's campus, to speak with the board. Thorpe gave them an overview of the activities of the Robotics Institute and examples of the military and commercial possibilities for robotics. He demonstrated a prototype of a small robot that was built on campus. Researchers were building larger robots at the National Robotics Engineering Center in Lawrenceville, he told them, but they were running short of space. To capture the emerging industry, Robinson said, the region had to find more space for entrepreneurs attempting to turn their ideas into companies with marketable products, or risk losing them. The board approved the purchase of the Heppenstall property, along with borrowing more money from the state, the local Strategic Investment Fund, and commercial banks to pay for its renovation.[9]

Redeveloping the former Geoffrey Boehm factory was the first project undertaken in what would become RIDC's Lawrenceville Technology Center. The 70,000-square-foot building was aptly named the Chocolate Factory. Seegrid, a three-year-old company, moved in as its first tenant in 2006. The company was co-founded by Hans Moravec, who came to Carnegie Mellon's Robotics Institute in 1980 as a research scientist. Discoveries at his Mobile Robot Lab had advanced the understanding of spatial awareness, which was critical to making mobile autonomous robots. Seegrid developed robots for handling materials in manufacturing and warehousing. RedZone Robotics was another early Chocolate Factory tenant. Founded by Carnegie Mellon's Whitaker, the company made autonomous robots capable of working underground to inspect storm and sanitary sewer systems. From its earliest days, the Chocolate Factory was earning a reputation as a place where tech companies could mature and succeed.

The Chocolate Factory had been open for three years, but not fully occupied with rent-paying tenants, when Donald Smith became RIDC president in 2009. It would take several more years for it to earn enough income to break even. On the nonprofit's neighboring property, most of the deteriorating Heppenstall Steel structures had been environmentally remediated and razed, with the exception of a 32,000-square-foot heavy manufacturing building, known as the "Blue Building." It was to be spared and renovated as office, lab, and high-bay manufacturing space, which in 2017 would be recognized as one of the best industrial redevelopment projects undertaken in the United States. Otherwise, the steelworks property remained undeveloped.

∼

Smith became RIDC president during a difficult year for the nation. The fallout from the Great Recession was deeply felt. Unemployment was spiking, banks were in crisis, and the housing market was in freefall. Southwestern Pennsylvania did not escape recession, but it fared better than most U.S. metropolitan regions. Its housing market, never prone to dramatic price swings, suffered less when the housing bubble burst nationwide, not having experienced much of a bubble in the first place. A more diverse local economy had replaced an overdependence on heavy manufacturing, and emerging strengths in health care, education, and technology helped soften the impact of the downturn. Pittsburgh was among the first metro regions in North America to see employment and gross-domestic-product per capita recover to pre-recession levels.[10] "I think our region is very well poised," Stuart Hoffman, chief economist for PNC Financial Services Group, the region's largest bank, told the nonprofit regional indicators project *Pittsburgh Today* in 2012. "We have a broader and more balanced job market and economic structure in southwestern Pennsylvania than we have had in a long time."[11]

Inside RIDC, completing the nonprofit's financial recovery was one of Smith's first challenges. "We had too much debt and not enough cash and a lot of underperforming properties that had a huge amount of deferred maintenance," Smith recalled. "And we weren't generating sufficient cash flow every year to change that." The nonprofit's financial condition was limiting its capacity to participate in projects, which didn't go unnoticed. "Who did the region go to when it wanted to save the Nabisco bakery? RIDC. Who did they go to to build the Pittsburgh Technology Center when [redeveloping] brownfields was something nobody knew how to do? Time and time again, the region turned to RIDC to address the big opportunity or need and RIDC answered.

Once we got into these cash-poor conditions and couldn't really do as many big projects, we were no longer viewed as the go-to partner. We had to figure out pretty quickly how to stop the bleeding, start generating some cash and reinvest in the facilities."

The internal accounting of the nonprofit's financial condition was refined. Each of its properties was reviewed and ranked by how they were performing. A handful of the poorest performing were found to be the biggest drag on RIDC's recovery. The nonprofit considered two options: find a way for those poor performers to at least break even on the balance sheet, or "give the keys back to the bank." None were returned to the bank. RIDC invested in improving poor performers that were considered marketable to make them more attractive to tenants. Other properties that were considered as less marketable were sold, more so to cut losses than to make a profit. A new approach to assessing potential projects was put in place that enabled the nonprofit to more thoroughly analyze building costs, operating expenses, debt, anticipated income, and other immediate and future financial aspects of a deal on the table. RIDC would still be willing to take on a degree of risk that would dissuade private developers, but the nonprofit would be more discerning when deciding which project to invest its limited resources in. Both the impact on the region and the financial viability of the project would be weighed. Preference would be given to those with the potential to be "catalytic" in terms of generating sustainable jobs and broad economic benefits. Even those would have to work financially, requiring a plan to fill any antici-pated gap in funding with public or foundation grants, or other funding sources. "It was marrying the economic development mission with the business of real estate," Smith explained.

Four years later, RIDC was turning the corner. Smith reported it ended 2012 with more than $155 million in assets against liabilities of nearly $102 million, including $77 million in debt. Revenue was $38.1 million, more than $25 million of which came from rent. Expenses came to nearly $27.5 million.[12] Some large debts, such as the mortgage owed to Westinghouse for the purchase of its East Pittsburgh plant, had been paid off. Fiscal 2013 was even better. Total debt and the nonprofit's debt-to-net-assets ratio fell to their lowest levels since 1999.[13] Occupancy rates were increasing at most of its properties. "By paring debt and right-sizing the portfolio, we have significantly improved our balance sheet," Smith told the board. "This is a key step in allowing us to exert a more aggressive development agenda to meet the region's needs."[14]

Attracting tenants to its Lawrenceville properties was not a concern. The Chocolate Factory was nearly full by 2014. The Heppenstall Blue Building was being readied for a promising robotics company that started in the National Robotics Engineering Center. Within two years, RIDC would build its Tech Forge nearby. The energy efficient, LEED-platinum-rated building introduced "tech-flex" design, which made it easily adaptable to a tenant's changing space requirements. Demand for such places was rising. More robotics companies were being founded as interest in machines smart enough to complete jobs on their own intensified.

ROBOTICS ROW

A team of journalists from GeekWire, a Seattle-based technology news site, settled in Pittsburgh for a month in 2018 to report on the local tech scene. Their chief reason for selecting Pittsburgh as its temporary second headquarters was "all the fascinating stuff to cover," ranging from robotics, artificial intelligence, and self-driving cars to the emergence of promising start-ups and the engineering centers Google, Microsoft, Apple, and other major technology companies established in the city years earlier.[15] The reporters spent February in Pittsburgh, one of the city's coldest, grayest, and least-flattering months of the year. A wiser decision was setting up shop in a co-working space in Lawrenceville. The neighborhood had become a launch pad for the tech entrepreneurs and companies fueling a fast-growing robotics and autonomous systems industry. By 2018, a cluster of companies was spreading from Lawrenceville to the Downtown border along a three-mile corridor that had become known as Robotics Row. They were catching the eye of investors and major companies eager to adopt their technologies, including Ford, ridesharing giant Uber, and Caterpillar, the world's largest maker of construction equipment.

In the 1990s, RIDC had recognized the abandoned industrial properties in Lawrenceville could become valuable in capturing the commercial potential of the nearby National Robotics Engineering Center. Twenty years later, RIDC was led by people who were familiar with the universities and experienced in creating conditions that support the commercialization of ideas flowing from them. They knew many of the key people in the local tech industry and understood the challenges start-ups encounter. Smith had led the economic development efforts of Carnegie Mellon and the University of Pittsburgh and been involved in establishing early tech incubators. Timothy White, RIDC senior vice president for business development and strategy, had worked with Smith in university economic development and had been a tech company executive. Board members included Audrey Russo, president and chief executive officer of the Pittsburgh Technology Council.

Among the hurdles that confronted young tech companies was finding an affordable home that suited their needs in a real estate market that often considered them risky tenants. Many early-stage companies didn't have a credit history that satisfied landlords, if they had one at all. Their founders may never have managed a company before. Their companies were often not generating enough income to cover the cost of their operations. What they needed in a building could change quickly, from enough office space for a few employees to a much larger plant with room for a substantial workforce, a large lab, and space for testing and manufacturing to execute a major contract.

RIDC opened its Lawrenceville Tech Forge in 2017. Less than a year later, three-quarters of the building had been leased to companies hungry for space,[16] joining the Chocolate Factory and the Blue Building on the Heppenstall Steel property as places where entrepreneurs and companies, several of them being risky bets as tenants, were finding the space they needed to prove their technologies and grow. "The rise of Robotics Row is as much about real estate as it is tech," GeekWire reported.[17] "A lot of these companies need big open spaces for research, development and testing. Pittsburgh's stock of old mills and factories provide ample opportunities for these companies to find the space they need."

～

RIDC's gamble that the National Robotics Engineering Center would become a catalyst for a new industry paid off. It quickly attracted top researchers, building a base of expertise in robotics before there was much of a robotics industry to speak of. Its research and the people doing it attracted companies keen on innovating their businesses, particularly in the field of self-driving vehicles. The National Robotics Engineering Center's top researchers had impressive resumes. Many of them were educated at Carnegie Mellon. Several had been involved with the school's Tartan Racing team, whose early autonomous vehicles were the stars of national field competitions organized by the Defense Advanced Research Projects Agency, the research arm of the U.S. Department of Defense. In those competitions, autonomous vehicles developed by leading computer science schools were judged on how they performed while navigating courses that replicated both open-road and urban settings. Automakers and other companies that saw autonomous systems in their future paid attention. Tartan Racing, consistently a top finisher, won the 2007 DARPA Urban Challenge with "Boss," a self-driving Chevrolet Tahoe sport utility vehicle. "Robots sometimes stun the world, inspire a lot of people and change the belief of what is possible," said Carnegie Mellon's Red Whittaker, leader of Tartan Racing, after the victory.[18] Entrepreneurs with the drive to create companies from their ideas emerged from the talent gathered in Lawrenceville. Companies spun out of the National Robotics Engineering Center in need of places to develop their businesses.

The Chocolate Factory was intended as an affordable place where early-stage companies could mature toward expansion. When Whittaker's start-up, RedZone Robotics, outgrew its space there, RIDC moved the company to its Thorn Hill suburban industrial park north of the City of Pittsburgh. When Seegrid outgrew the Chocolate Factory, it moved to RIDC Park West near Pittsburgh International Airport to expand its business. New start-ups looking to launch replaced those that departed.

Among them was Carnegie Robotics. The company was founded in 2010 by John Bares, who had left the National Robotics Engineering Center, where he had been the director for longer than a decade, to start a company that would commercialize the robotics concepts developed in the lab. "At NREC, too often we did proof of concepts and handed them to a customer and they would say, 'What am I supposed to do? I wanted product.' They had to go find a third party. We'd call it, 'throwing it over the fence.' If our customer couldn't find a third party, it would just die. I wanted to be the third party." Bares and a few colleagues who joined him had little money between them to invest in their company. They had no financial backers. No customers lined up. Conventional work space at the National Robotics Engineering Center was filled, but Carnegie Mellon allowed them to work out of makeshift offices built from shipping containers. "And we put up two huge office trailers outside, which were eyesores, and we took some heat over that." Landing a couple of government contracts provided them with some money to shop for a place of their own, preferably something affordable within a two-mile radius of the National Robotics Engineering Center. Their search proved fruitless.

Bares was in the hospital recovering from back surgery in 2012 when he got a phone call from a number he did not recognize. "A guy said, 'I'm Tim White. I'm with RIDC.' I'm like, 'What is RIDC?' He said, 'I heard you were looking for some space,'" Bares recalled. White asked whether Bares had considered the blue building that had been part of the Heppenstall steelworks and was located next door to the National Robotics Engineering Center. "In my mind, I'm thinking the thing is the size of an aircraft carrier. What's he talking about? I said, 'Tim, we're like 10 people. I appreciate the location. It would be perfect. But we're tiny.' He said, 'Let's talk. Maybe we can work with you.' It was a pivotal moment. He could've said, 'What, you're only 10 people?' Click."

Carnegie Robotics took temporary quarters in the Chocolate Factory while RIDC built out the Heppenstall Steel Blue Building as a permanent home for the company with the high-bay space it sought. RIDC used its equity, a revolving loan fund it had established with foundation support and state funding to finance the build-out. Carnegie Robotics contributed several million dollars toward improving the building as well. The Carnegie Robotics workforce increased to some 150 employees as its client list grew, which included the U.S. Department of Defense.

The military's interest in robotic solutions to dangerous situations led to several contracts, including one for robots that can detect and mark land mines and other buried explosives. The company's success added to the momentum of the robotics cluster forming in the city. "We took a risk," White said of RIDC's decision to invest in building out the Blue Building. "But our thinking at the time was, if this company doesn't work out, these guys or someone else is going to create another company. Not every bet works. But that one did."

Around the same time, Ragunathan "Raj" Rajkumar, a Tartan Racing veteran who would become George Westinghouse Professor of Electrical and Computer Engineering at Carnegie Mellon, was testing autonomous vehicles at Hazelwood Green. He started Ottomatika, an autonomous systems developer, in 2013. When the company expanded, it moved to RIDC's O'Hara park. Ottomatika was acquired by Delphi, a global supplier of vehicle electronics, which was rebranded as Aptiv. Aptiv, in a joint venture with South Korean automaker Hyundai, formed an autonomous vehicle company, Motional, which placed its Pittsburgh operations in RIDC's Mill 19 in Hazelwood.

Meanwhile, with renovations nearly complete, Carnegie Robotics was about to move into the renovated Heppenstall Steel Blue Building in Lawrenceville. Bares, however, would not be moving in with it. The company had received an email inquiry from the ridesharing company, Uber, asking whether Carnegie Robotics had any interest in exploring self-driving vehicles. Paying its drivers was the Silicon Valley company's biggest expense. Bares recalled that Uber co-founder Travis Kalanick was "passionate that he was going to do self-driving in Pittsburgh" and compete against Google, which was the leader in the field at the time. Carnegie Robotics and Uber formed Uber ATG (Advanced Technologies Group) in 2015. The structure of the deal came together in little more than two weeks. Bares became its founding director.

White recalled receiving a phone call from the Carnegie Robotics chief financial officer on the day before Thanksgiving, 2015: "Tim, we're going to sign this huge deal. We're going to need to be in a space as soon as possible. Can we do it in 30 days?" White responded that he "couldn't get a permit for anything in 30 days." But room had opened up in the Chocolate Factory. A lease was signed that weekend. As many as 50 Carnegie Mellon scientists and engineers were hired to lucrative jobs to establish the research core of Uber ATG. They moved into the Chocolate Factory several months later. "The cars in the parking lot were more valuable than the building," White remembered thinking. Uber ATG tested its technologies at a track built at Hazelwood Green. Later, RIDC built the company another test track at its Westmoreland County industrial park. Uber ATG scaled up quickly. "We were hiring people about every single day," Bares recalled. "It was like a rocket ship." Before long, the Chocolate Factory could no longer hold the growing company. With its payroll swelling toward 1,000 employees, Uber ATG moved westward within Robotics Row to the city's Strip District neighborhood bordering Downtown.

After Uber ATG moved out of the Chocolate Factory, Aurora Innovation moved in. The California autonomous vehicle developer had roots in Pittsburgh. Its founders included Chris Urmson, who had led Google's self-driving project. Urmson had earned his doctorate in robotics at Carnegie Mellon and had been director of technology for the Tartan Racing team. Another Aurora co-founder, Drew Bagnell, was Urmson's Tartan Racing teammate and a Carnegie Mellon professor who had worked for Uber ATG. Aurora, too, was growing and soon moved from the Chocolate Factory into RIDC's Tech Forge in Lawrenceville, which it shared with Caterpillar's Automation Engineering Center, a unit of the international corporation that applies autonomous technologies to construction and other heavy equipment. In 2020, Aurora acquired Uber ATG and began generating headlines for its plan to put autonomous long-haul trucks on the highway. "Suddenly, you have multiple big players in town with deep pockets," White said.

The breathtaking potential of machines that can operate cars and machinery on their own made autonomous systems a hot technology that carmakers, in particular, scrambled to invest in. Companies within Robotics Row were raising billions of dollars to develop their ideas. They were not, however, immune to the setbacks that companies developing groundbreaking technologies can encounter. Pittsburgh-based Argo AI, founded in 2016 by National Robotics Engineering Center alumni Bryan

Salesky and Peter Rander, raised more than $3 billion to develop high-level autonomous vehicle systems for Ford and Volkswagen. Six years later, the company closed when the automakers backed out, concerned about lingering uncertainty over when the technology would be ready for commercial use, as well as the uncertain U.S. regulatory environment for driverless vehicles.[19] About one year after Argo AI closed, Salesky and Rander found an investor in Japan's Softbank to fund the launch of a new start-up, Stack AV, which became the second Pittsburgh-based company to focus on autonomous trucking. A critical stage in determining the commercial viability of autonomous long-haul trucking would come in 2024, when Aurora announced that for the first time its semi-trucks would begin traveling Texas highways on their own without a human safety driver standing by in the jump seat.[20]

~

The city's Lawrenceville neighborhood underwent a dramatic transformation. Declining population and few newcomers had rendered its population one of the oldest in the city. From 1970 to 1990, the concentration of residents aged 65 years or older had soared to more than 25 percent of the neighborhood's population. Several sections of the neighborhood had become what is known as Naturally Occurring Retirement Communities, a demographic term for areas that were not originally planned to harbor such large numbers of seniors aging in place. Empty storefronts had multiplied along Butler Street, the neighborhood's main thoroughfare. In 1995, the median sale price for a house in Lawrenceville had slipped to $35,094. Conditions slowly began to improve, coinciding with the opening of the National Robotics Engineering Center, the neighborhood's rise as a hub of technology innovation and the work of community organizations, which focused on real estate development, recruiting businesses, improving the business district, reducing crime, and removing blight.[21]

Lawrenceville became markedly younger, more hip than working-class, and a place where a house selling for $35,000 or less was unimaginable. Once-empty storefronts attracted art galleries and inspired restauranteurs to open new culinary destinations. The median price of a house doubled by 2010.[22] Seven years later, it reached $237,000,[23] more than six times the 1970 median price. Seniors accounted for only 16 percent of the population in 2010.[24] Six years later, as many as 42 percent of people living in Lawrenceville had been born during the last two decades of the 20th century, the first generation to grow up with the Internet. "Once a pass-through neighborhood known for blight and crime in the 1990s, Lawrenceville has emerged as one of Pittsburgh's fastest growing areas and is attracting millennials in droves," the *Pittsburgh City Paper* reported.[25]

THE FOREFRONT REPORT

It became increasingly difficult not to notice the rise of robotics in the City of Pittsburgh. More and more companies appeared on the landscape. They consumed much of the available commercial real estate in the Lawrenceville and Strip District neighborhoods and began trickling into Hazelwood. Local news media reported the potential wonders of autonomous technologies and the enormous sums of investors' dollars that start-ups developing those technologies were attracting. The innovation corridor was christened Robotics Row. National media took note, some even going as far as calling Pittsburgh "Roboburgh"[26] or "Robocity." Self-driving cars with their whirring roof-mounted sensors were routinely spotted on city streets, albeit with human drivers as passengers to prevent mishaps during test runs. Yet, while it was apparent an industry cluster around mobile autonomous technology was taking shape, local government and economic development officials lacked a firm understanding of what was happening. There was no plan for supporting the sector, for expanding it, or for leveraging the technologies to generate jobs well into the future. RIDC, the largest landlord for autonomous companies in the region, was concerned the opportunity, if ignored, could slip away or at least be diminished. Smith advocated for a proactive approach. He found an ally in Sam Reiman, director of the Richard King Mellon Foundation, the largest philanthropic organization in the city with assets of more than $3.4 billion.

"I went to Sam Reiman," Smith recalled, "and said, I have been talking to the economic development leaders in town for five years, saying we have this opportunity. We have these autonomy companies. We need to bring in their suppliers, their customers, figure out how we can double their presence in the region. We need to talk to them. We need to put together a plan. And people would go, 'yes, we do.' Five years later, nothing has been done." The Richard King Mellon Foundation provided a grant that enabled RIDC, with the Greater Pittsburgh Chamber of Commerce as a partner, to lead a study that would inventory the local mobile autonomous cluster, survey companies to learn the necessary ingredients for their success, assess the national competition, and offer a strategy for expanding and sustaining the sector in southwestern Pennsylvania and extending its reach to benefit other industries and a wider swath of people and places.

The market for autonomous mobile systems was projected to be substantial. The study, "Forefront: Securing Pittsburgh's Break-out Position in Autonomous Mobile Systems," estimated the global market for land-based systems alone would exceed $800 billion by 2026. When aerial, marine, and defense autonomous systems were added, the market climbed above $1 trillion. Capturing 1 percent of that market could bring $10 billion over five-plus years and an estimated 5,000 jobs to a region with the technology stack required by such systems.

Pittsburgh was well-positioned to pursue such riches, the study found. The region had become "one of the distinct hubs for autonomous systems activity in the country." The local ecosystem had begun to drive an industry cluster of emerging and established companies. Central to the maturation of the innovation ecosystem were the region's universities, producers of high-level talent and advanced research that "reflect a history of excellence in the underlying technologies that now support full stack autonomy development and testing."[27] The study, released in 2021, counted 60 mobile autonomous systems companies in the Pittsburgh area at the time. It was enough to give Pittsburgh the seventh-largest cluster in the country—a list dominated by California's Silicon Valley, where nearly 450 autonomous systems companies resided. Major companies made up more than 38 percent of Pittsburgh's autonomy cluster, one of the largest proportions of industry leaders in the country.

As rapidly as the promising industry cluster had grown, it had its shortcomings, the study noted. There were concerns about whether Pennsylvania could create a regulatory environment that would allow the autonomy industry to attract investment and grow. Local sources of venture capital were limited. Autonomous companies and others identified the "lack of ecosystem coordination" as a risk. Although the Pittsburgh Robotics Network focused on garnering support for growing the cluster, the nonprofit's resources were limited. More infrastructure for testing autonomous systems was needed. Another concern was that the region was viewed as an "R&D outpost" by some major companies rather than a headquarters destination or a place to locate manufacturing and other operations that would generate larger numbers of jobs and more diverse job opportunities.

The Forefront report offered a comprehensive strategy for improving the competitive standing of southwestern Pennsylvania's budding mobile autonomous industry. It included taking steps from promoting the region as a leading autonomy hub to enhancing support for entrepreneurs, building out contract manufacturing and the regional supply chain, building shared autonomous vehicle testing tracks and coordinating efforts across educational institutions to expand the talent pipeline. The report also issued a warning: "If the Pittsburgh region maintains its current market share and innovation ecosystem but does not take significant action to improve its competitive position, it may be able to continue to grow organically, but is not likely to attract a significant share of these new jobs that can accelerate the growth of the cluster beyond its current R&D-focused employment footprint. In the face of competition from other states for these new jobs . . . there is no guarantee that Pittsburgh will be the primary destination for ongoing growth as [autonomous vehicle] companies seek to find attractive environments to site their new business functions."[28]

∽

Less than two months after he took office in 2021, President Joe Biden signed the American Rescue Plan Act into law, authorizing the spending of $1.9 trillion to shore up the U.S. economy in the wake of the COVID-19 pandemic. As part of the plan, the government invited regions to compete for grants to develop and strengthen local industry clusters under the $1 billion Build Back Better Challenge. The deadline was tight—eight months to draft a proposal that identified regional assets, was aligned with industry needs, and included a plan to maintain or improve the cluster's growth and broadly share the benefits it generates. Winning initiatives would receive grants ranging from $25 million to $65 million.[29] In Pittsburgh, a group calling itself the Southwestern Pennsylvania New Economy Collaborative quickly formed to draft the region's proposal. Its partners included representatives of universities, business, labor, economic development organizations, and others.

The timing was fortuitous. The Forefront report had just been completed. The coalition had a blueprint in hand. The report became the "framing document" for the region's proposal, Reiman recalled. "We had thought it would help inform our thinking about new ways to support emerging robotics and autonomous companies, research and the physical facilities these types of companies need. What we couldn't anticipate was that the results of the study would leverage funding from the federal government to support autonomous research and robotics industries in the region." Twenty-one regional coalitions were awarded grants out of the 529 that submitted proposals. Southwestern Pennsylvania was one of them, receiving $62.7 million to support the coalition's plan for building out the robotics and autonomy cluster in the region.

Several regional projects would be financed with the grant money. Local organizations would help implement them, including RIDC. The projects generally reflected the findings of the Forefront report. One would create an Applied Robotics Startup Factory to help start-ups mature that are focused on bringing robotics and automation to other industries, including agriculture, construction, manufacturing, and energy. Another would establish a coordinated system for advancing the skills of robotics technology developers and employees of companies adopting robotics technology, and offer training options that do not require four-year or advanced college degrees. RIDC and the Advanced Robotics for Manufacturing Institute—Mill 19's anchor tenant—would help build the capacity of organizations in five counties to support manufacturing entrepreneurs and small and medium-sized companies adopt advanced robotics and automation technologies. At the same time, RIDC and its partners were advancing plans to build a test track that could be shared by universities, companies, and state agencies working on transportation-related autonomous systems. Together, the projects addressed many of the concerns raised in the Forefront report that despite the region's emergence as a potent hub of robotics and autonomy research, it could fail to capture the full potential of the innovations flowing from it. "We have a budding industry," White said. "The question is, how can we grow it to where it translates into manufacturing, which is the real gravy in terms of jobs and capital investment."

Transferring the emerging technologies to manufacturing would also improve the chances of stimulating employment beyond the confines of Robotics Row, including surrounding counties, where factory jobs have been disappearing in recent decades.

Truly Regional

The Region's Connector

More than 1,200 acres of rolling farmland in Westmoreland County near the New Stanton Pennsylvania Turnpike interchange made national news in the fall of 1968. "Farm Area to Get Plant of Chrysler," read the headline above a story in the *New York Times* reporting the Detroit-based automaker's decision to build an auto assembly plant there that would employ some 4,000 workers with an annual payroll of $40 million. "The Chrysler plant, in view of knowledgeable area developers, is the biggest new industry in the Pittsburgh district since the end of World War II. Pittsburgh notably missed the automobile industry and this will be the district's first plant to turn out complete cars."[1] It was a triumph for the county that borders Allegheny to the east, one expected to "cause all of the usual results of a new plant constructed in farmland: new housing and satellite industries that supply components to auto assembly plants." Chrysler never made a single car at its new plant. The smallest of the nation's Big Three automakers, it was already struggling to compete against the low-cost, fuel-efficient imports entering the U.S. market when it broke ground in Westmoreland County. Two years after announcing its arrival to great fanfare, Chrysler abandoned its plans.[2] The sprawling factory shell it left unfinished would remain empty for nearly eight years until it caught the eye of one of the U.S. automaker's foreign competitors searching for a place to build its cars on American soil.

The 2.8 million square foot facility in Westmoreland County employed as many as 3,000 workers as a plant for Volkswagen and then Sony Corporation until the Sony plant closed in 2010 (top). In partnership with the Westmoreland County Industrial Development Corporation, RIDC has revitalized the facility, now called the Westmoreland Innovation Center, into a multi-tenant, high-growth manufacturing hub. Current tenants include Siemens Energy, Intervala, City Brewery, and Westmoreland County Community College's Advanced Technology Center.

The property will also become home to PennSTART, a project that responds to the needs of the autonomous technology industry to have a shared research facility and state-of-the-art test track in the region. The PennSTART partnership includes the Pennsylvania Department of Transportation, Turnpike Commission, Westmoreland County, and Carnegie Mellon University and will also serve as a training facility for first responders (bottom).

Pennsylvania governor Milton Shapp and state lawmakers offered Volkswagen an incentive package in 1976 that the German automaker did not refuse: $100 million in state assistance, tax exemptions, and highway and rail improvements to make the empty Westmoreland County factory the first foreign-owned auto assembly plant in the United States.[3] In return, Volkswagen did what Chrysler had only promised. It made cars at the Westmoreland plant, turning out as many as 200,000 of its Rabbit diesel-engine model a year. The plant employed 2,500 workers on average and as many as 5,700 during its most productive years.[4] It also drew local manufacturers into its supply chain. Among them was a PPG Industries glass plant in South Greensburg eight miles away, where Ray Maffit had taken a job fresh out of high school. PPG made windshields for the Volkswagen Rabbit, indirectly connecting Maffit to the star-crossed Westmoreland auto plant around which his career would revolve for decades.

Less than 10 years after its first cars rolled off the assembly line, Volkswagen announced it was closing its Westmoreland County factory. The automaker, whose officials had spoken confidently of capturing 5 percent of the U.S. car market, had managed to capture less than 2 percent. "VW Westmoreland has been operating at less than half its designed capacity for the past five years," the company explained in 1987.[5] After years of seeing jobs increase by the thousands, Westmoreland County found itself on the downside of the boom-or-bust cycle that comes as a risk when betting on large employers. "Volkswagen, at its height, had more than 5,000 jobs at that site. That's a significant number to lose. But with a facility of that size, scale and magnitude, it's not just the jobs on site, it's also the indirect jobs—the contracts they have with local companies and vendors, the money that flows into the community," said Jason Rigone, executive director of the Westmoreland County Industrial Development Corporation. "When all of a sudden one day they announce they are leaving, there is a substantial economy impact that ripples through the community." The company's local supply chain was not spared the pain of losing a major customer. PPG closed its South Greensburg plant six years later, eliminating hundreds of jobs. Maffit, however, managed to land on his feet.

After standing empty for two years, the former Volkswagen plant attracted the interest of Sony, the Japanese electronics giant, which had been searching the East Coast for a suitable place to manufacture one million television picture tubes a year that would be shipped to the company's assembly plant in San Diego, California, governor Robert P. Casey had identified finding a new tenant for the Westmoreland plant that the state had heavily invested in as the "No. 1 economic priority" in Pennsylvania[6] and was willing to deal. Sony chose Westmoreland County in 1990, accepting nearly $24 million in low-interest state loans and negotiating a 20-year lease with the state that totaled $21 million. The fact Sony didn't have to build a plant worked in the county's favor in the competition with other regions, including Columbus, Ohio, and northern Kentucky near Cincinnati. Southwestern Pennsylvania "fits our needs ideally with an excellent skilled workforce, good transportation channels and an outstanding manufacturing tradition," Masaaki Morita, chairman of Sony Corporation of America, told the *Pittsburgh Press*, "We view this decision as a significant, long-term investment in the economic future of the Pittsburgh area." Maffit took a job with Sony, working first as facility mechanic, then as a facility engineer. By 2010, circumstances would force him to look for another job, again.

RIDC had "worked confidentially" with the nonprofit Penn's Southwest in 1989 to help bring Sony's East Coast television tube factory to the abandoned Volkswagen plant.[7] A decade earlier, RIDC had helped to establish a foreign trade subzone, which allowed companies engaged in international commerce to pay reduced customs duties, taxes, and fees—or to avoid them altogether—on goods moving into and out of the country.[8] Sony soon revived the rural plant and county's economic prospects. The company expanded its footprint, building its own on-site glass factory. The television plant employed as many as 3,000 workers, most of them local. The highly automated operation with its advanced equipment and skilled workforce stood "at the forefront of the global economy" and made the American manufacturing base "much stronger," U.S. Treasury Secretary John W. Snow remarked while touring the plant in 2005.[9]

Sony decided to leave Westmoreland County three years later, closing its last U.S. manufacturing operation. An increasing number of competitors offering quality flat-screen televisions at lower prices, the onset of the Great Recession, and a strong yen were among the circumstances battering company profits.[10] As Sony began to restructure its global operations in response, the company warned the Pennsylvania Industrial Development Authority, owner of the Westmoreland plant, that it would not renew its lease beyond 2010, when it was due to expire. Maffit watched as the equipment that for nearly two decades made up to two million rear-projection and LCD televisions a year was packed, loaded onto rail cars, and shipped to the company's Baja, Mexico, plant, which took over the company's production for the U.S. market. Nearly all of the remaining 560 workers lost their jobs. Maffit was not one of them. Without losing a paycheck, he moved to a new job at the plant: senior site manager for its new owners, RIDC and the Westmoreland County Industrial Development Corporation, a partnership looking to preserve local manufacturing and extend the innovation corridor from Pittsburgh's universities and blossoming technology sector farther out into the region.

A REGIONAL FOOTPRINT

Sony's departure left the largest manufacturing site in southwestern Pennsylvania wanting for tenants. Sony had left behind a temporary television refurbishing operation. Two small tenants and two larger ones had moved onto the site, including a maker of thermal transfer ribbons used in printers. But most of the 2.8 million square feet that was available under roof was empty. The state's investment in the plant and surrounding infrastructure was at risk, again, and at the same time, providing fewer jobs. Donald Smith had been the president of RIDC for less than one year when PIDA officials asked the nonprofit to consider drafting a business model, redevelop the plant for new tenants, manage it, and assume the financial risks going forward.[11, 12]

Taking on a property that large was a risky proposition for RIDC, leading the nonprofit to arrange a partnership with the Westmoreland County Industrial Development Corporation to tackle the project. The square footage involved was more than five times greater than what the Westmoreland County Industrial Development Corporation had in its entire portfolio of buildings and industrial parks. RIDC was working to strengthen its balance sheet after acquiring substantial debt redeveloping abandoned industrial plants in the Mon Valley that took a decade or, in several cases, much longer to generate enough income to cover operating expenses. The nonprofit had recently been making progress paring its debt, and its board was concerned about adding to it. Redeveloping the former Sony plant would be a challenge, financially and otherwise. "If we had taken Sony and put $30 million into it and it didn't work, it could've put us under," Smith recalled.

Unlike the older steel mills RIDC redeveloped in Allegheny County, demolition at the Westmoreland site was unnecessary. But a whopping 50 acres of roof would need to be replaced within five to seven years. Both parties agreed that redeveloping the vast plant for multiple tenants rather than for a single, large user for which it had been designed was the prudent strategy to pursue. That would require elaborate redesign. It stood as one cavernous building serviced by a central utility plant. While heating and cooling the entire building may have worked for Volkswagen and Sony, it was an inefficient, wasteful approach to serving a building that would be broken into smaller spaces, some of which might be unoccupied at any point in time. Utilities had to be decentralized. RIDC would have to figure out how to reconfigure the building so each tenant was positioned close enough to fire-rated corridors to meet state safety codes. If the daunting prospect of redeveloping it wasn't enough, there was the market to consider. It was 35 miles from Pittsburgh and 55 miles from Pittsburgh International Airport, the region's largest. South-central Westmoreland County, where it was located, was sparsely populated and had few businesses compared to Allegheny County, the region's commercial hub. Whether the repurposed site could attract enough small-to-medium-sized tenants, and perhaps start-ups and early-stage companies, to make it financially viable was an open question.

On the other hand, the highway, rail, gas, and water infrastructure serving the site was considered exceptional. Making the request was PIDA, the site owner, which had been a key source of financial support on other RIDC projects for decades. The proposal was to redevelop and manage the plant and about 300 acres, leaving another nearly 900 acres of surrounding state-owned land for additional development, if warranted. Reviving the largest available industrial site in southwestern Pennsylvania would benefit the regional economy, which aligned with the nonprofit's half-century-old mission. The site already had a few rent-paying tenants. In the Westmoreland County Industrial Development Corporation, RIDC found a partner whose portfolio, although lighter than RIDC's, demonstrated it was capable of holding up its end of the bargain, and which was willing to share the financial risks the project posed. RIDC decided to take on the project with the Westmoreland County agency and started laying the groundwork for redeveloping the plant two years before a deal with the state was signed.[13, 14] "The one thing that swung it was the cooperation of the county commissioners and the economic development organization in Westmoreland County— their understanding of what a partnership would look like," recalled Reynolds Clark, chairman of the RIDC board of directors at the time. "Some partnerships don't work because there is one partner who expects the other to do the work. Partnerships work when everybody pitches in and understands the risk and is willing to move forward. That was the case in Westmoreland." Redeveloping the former Sony plant was also an opportunity for RIDC to explore how it could become what Smith described as a "truly regional" economic development organization.

~

RIDC had begun revisiting its approach to economic development shortly after Smith became president. A survey of the board of directors, a "goals team" made up of board members, and other information-gathering steps were taken as part of the strategic planning process. The questions explored centered around what the appropriate role for RIDC should be, what level of financial risk it should assume, and how it works with regional partners, private developers, and government. Taking a more regional approach had been gaining momentum. Engaging with partners on major projects was becoming a necessity. Both were influenced by political and economic realities that were different than when RIDC was undertaking its early suburban industrial parks and redeveloping shuttered industrial plants. Beginning in the 21st century, for example, the federal government largely shifted away from awarding block grants and other direct funding to help attract private investment to distressed communities in favor of awarding credits against an investor's future federal tax obligations. But tax credits did little to overcome private sector hesitancy over investing in places such as the Mon Valley, where the market was weak and the future was clouded in uncertainty. More concerning for RIDC was a trend that saw Pennsylvania economic development funding becoming more scarce and increasingly difficult to obtain. RIDC no longer had near-exclusive access to low-interest PIDA loans, which had made its most challenging redevelopment projects financially palatable. The state's broadening of eligibility to include private developers made the loans more competitive and diminished the chances of borrowing sums as large as those RIDC had borrowed for many major projects in the past. The lingering shortfall dropped Pennsylvania behind several neighboring states in the amount of funding earmarked for economic development, including Ohio, where financial incentives to attract and grow businesses would be seven times greater than what was available in the Commonwealth by 2023.[15]

Expanding its role in southwestern Pennsylvania and its presence in counties outside of Allegheny emerged as leading goals RIDC would pursue. The nonprofit in past years had done developments in most of the counties in the region, including the Hopewell Industrial Park in Beaver County, where the mass closure of its steel mills had crippled the economy; the Pullman Center in Butler County bordering Allegheny to the north; Meadow Ridge in Greene County near the state line shared with West Virginia; a park in mostly rural Armstrong County west of Allegheny; and Neshannock Business Park in Lawrence County, the region's northern-most county. Allegheny County, however, had commanded most of RIDC's attention and resources. More than half of the region's population resided in Allegheny County and the City of Pittsburgh within it. It was where RIDC was created. It was the center of commerce and employment and where the largest corporations had their headquarters. It had the largest concentration of steel mills and industrial plants in need of rescue when heavy manufacturing collapsed in the 1980s. The City of Pittsburgh was home to the region's research universities, the hotbeds of innovation that inspired an unprecedented number of new technology companies with the potential to develop into the economic engines of the future.

It was becoming clear to RIDC officials, however, that if the innovation rising from Pittsburgh's research corridor was to stimulate renewed demand for manufacturing, the demand would have to be met elsewhere, and outlying municipalities and counties were the likely candidates. "There's a notion that tech is only for the city," Smith said. "But you can't manufacture in the city today. Costs are too high. Regulations are too high. Traffic is too much of a problem. You need that symbiotic relationship. Maybe the [research and development] hubs are going to be in the city. But the job creation on a large scale is going to happen outside of the city, where you have the space for the one-story buildings, the parking lots, transportation access, cheaper power and lower rates for other things that are important to manufacturing."

Expanding its reach was coupled with an emphasis on seeking out partnerships with other economic development agencies, municipalities, and even private developers to help move new projects forward and ease the financial risks involved. RIDC and private developers had a tense relationship after the nonprofit began pursuing projects as a commercial developer in the early 1960s. Developers had argued RIDC enjoyed an unfair advantage by having access to low-interest state loans that for many years were not available to them. RIDC countered that for-profit developers only expressed interest in projects where the path to success was clear and that they avoided riskier, more difficult projects, such as redeveloping closed and contaminated steel mills and factories. RIDC moved to repair those relationships under Smith's administration. The nonprofit engaged in joint ventures with private developers. It started using private leasing agents to market some of its properties. Smith joined the National Association for Industrial and Office Parks, a commercial development trade group, eventually becoming a member of its national board.

As part of its strategy going forward, RIDC would marshal its resources more selectively, focusing on "catalytic" projects that stood the best chance of stimulating economic growth beyond the sites it developed by demonstrating new markets and creating supply chains to serve them, which nearly all of its board members felt should be the most important consideration.[16] Under a "seedling communities" initiative, the nonprofit would support the revitalization of economically distressed boroughs and cities where there were reasonable prospects for growth, such as assets on which to build, and local leaders and partners who demonstrated the will to engage in renewal but lacked the expertise and resources to carry it out on their own.[17]

The new course RIDC set out would bring internal changes. Payroll would grow to more than 30 employees, the largest staff to work for the nonprofit. RIDC, which had long avoided the public spotlight, would hire its first communications director, Steven Alschuler, a veteran public relations strategist who had moved to Pittsburgh after selling his interest in a New York–based firm he co-founded. The circumstances that led Smith to bring in a communications specialist were decidedly less dire than those that had confronted some of Alschuler's previous clients, which included Lehman Brothers Holdings following its global bankruptcy and the New Orleans public school system in the wake of Hurricane Katrina. But Smith found it unsettling that after six decades, RIDC was still "grotesquely misunderstood," even in Allegheny County, where most of its work had taken place. RIDC's public profile was in need of elevation now that it was more earnestly exploring projects and partnerships in places where it historically had little presence. Negotiations with state legislators, county commissioners, local economic development agencies, and other potential partners would be more fruitful, Smith reasoned, if they were aware of RIDC's accomplishments and understood its mission and the advantages it brought to the table.

RIDC added muscle to its economic development strategy and analysis capabilities as its geographic reach and standing as an influential voice in determining the course of the regional economy grew. A five-person team was assembled as the thinking piece of economic development. Among the team's assignments was quantifying the impact that the nonprofit's development projects were having on communities where they were located, including direct and indirect jobs created and local taxes generated. Other assignments included identifying global, national, and local trends and opportunities for growth among industries in the regional market, and determining what specific communities and counties needed to stimulate development within their borders and how RIDC could help. The team's work would contribute to the Forefront report that laid out a strategy for growing the promising cluster of autonomous systems companies forming in the region, the successful bid for a federal Build Back Better Challenge grant to support the local autonomous and robotics industries, and a strategy that would bring Pennsylvania's largest mobile autonomous systems testing complex to the site of the former Sony plant in Westmoreland County.

WESTMORELAND INNOVATION CENTER
RIDC took control of the former Sony plant in 2012 under a long-term lease with the state that included an option to buy. In a partnership arrangement with the Westmoreland County Industrial Development Corporation, RIDC would oversee the redevelopment and management of the site and assume the largest share of a 75 percent-to-25 percent split of any profits earned or any losses incurred. The partners shared a vision of remodeling the plant for multiple small-to-midsized companies, an approach each had successfully taken when developing their own industrial parks. Neither partner saw a moonshot approach of pursuing another single, large company as a practical consideration. Having a diverse mix of tenants tends to "add stability and consistency to our economy," Rigone said. "If one or two of them move out, that is something we can absorb." Losing a single, large tenant would be felt more broadly across the economy, and finding a replacement would likely mean engaging in challenging, expensive competition with other suitors within and outside the state.

Financing the redevelopment was a challenge. Commercial banks had little interest in financing a plant that large. It helped that the Commonwealth of Pennsylvania had a significant financial stake in the Westmoreland site's success. Despite the tightening of state economic development assistance, the project over time managed to secure nearly $23 million in PIDA loans and loans from the state's Business in Our Sites program intended to attract businesses to existing, but underused, sites.[18] It was also awarded a $10 million grant from the state Regional Capital Assistance Program, which funds economic improvement projects. The costs of reimagining 2.8 million square feet as a community of small and medium-sized companies was considerable. As a single-tenant plant, shipping had been located on one end and receiving on the other. Having multiple tenants meant redesigning the floor plan so each had its own shipping and receiving areas. The plant had to be divided in half with a broad, truck-accommodating corridor, to give each tenant the exits and entrances necessary to satisfy fire safety codes. Utilities were decoupled from the central plant to serve individual companies. As it had done at Keystone Commons and other previous projects, RIDC built out in stages to accommodate existing tenants and newly recruited ones, rather than redevelop the site all at once.

The first new tenant recruited by the partners was the Westmoreland County Community College, which signed a deal to place its Advanced Technology Training Center in the former Sony plant. The community college took 73,000 square feet where television circuit boards had once been assembled and converted it into labs and classrooms to train students for middle-skill jobs in technology-heavy fields, such as technicians in robotics, 3-D printing, and maintenance, repair, and modification of complex electronic systems.[19] Another early recruit, Aquion Energy, moved its manufacturing of saltwater batteries and storage systems from the City of Pittsburgh's Lawrenceville neighborhood, where the company had been co-founded by a Carnegie Mellon professor. In 2016, RIDC reached agreement with the German company, Siemens, to place its turbine generator reconditioning unit in a portion of the Westmoreland plant where Sony had made television tubes. Prior to the deal, Siemens planned to move the operation, which had started in RIDC's Keystone Commons industrial park, to North Carolina. An existing tenant, Dai Nippon Printing America, was experiencing a surge in demand for its thermal printer ribbons and expanded its footprint in the part of the plant where Sony had a chemical operation and extended its lease by 10 years.[20]

One year after RIDC agreed to take control of the former Sony plant, the industrial park it was developing there stood as the poorest performer of the properties in its portfolio with tenants occupying less than 28 percent of the available square footage.[21] Interest was steady, however, and the multiple-tenant industrial property demonstrated the resilience the developers hoped it would, recovering when tenants would exit, including Aquion Energy, which left after it was acquired in 2017. More than three-quarters of the industrial park was occupied in 2024. The companies there employed about 1,200 workers. And the Westmoreland Innovation Center was expanding as it prepared to play a key role in the development of the region's autonomous systems industry.

～

With the rapid development of autonomous mobile systems technologies in southwestern Pennsylvania came heightened demand for places and infrastructure that enable researchers to test them in real-world situations as a necessary step toward commercialization. Such sites were particularly important to the development of self-driving cars and trucks, which were constrained by regulation and safety concerns from being tested on the public streets and highways they aspired to travel. Closed test tracks were in short supply in the region and across Pennsylvania. Demand for places to demonstrate and test was expected to increase as the technologies moved closer to market. RIDC became aware of the pressing need for testing infrastructure through conversations with autonomous systems developers, many of whom were tenants at the nonprofit's properties. Several companies were looking outside of Lawrenceville for places that would allow them to test and trim their costs.[22] Addressing the shortage of testing areas was identified as a strategy critical to exploiting local innovations in autonomous systems in the RIDC-led Forefront study, which had gotten the attention of state economic development and transportation agencies.[23] The City of Pittsburgh, where most of the research and autonomous systems companies were located, did not have the open space suitable for a large-scale, advanced testing campus, such as those that were underway in Ohio and Michigan. The Westmoreland Innovation Center, with vast tracts of undeveloped state-owned land, did.

Pennsylvania officials responded in 2022, announcing that $22 million in public funds would be invested in creating the state's largest autonomous systems testing campus, known as PennSTART, at the former Sony plant. RIDC agreed to manage the site and, with the Westmoreland County Industrial Development Corporation as its partner, share in the cost of building and operating it.[24] Carnegie Mellon University would bring technological expertise to the project. The Pennsylvania Department of Transportation and state Turnpike Commission were interested in PennSTART as a proving ground for safety enhancement technologies, particularly those that could be deployed in highway work zones. From 2013 through 2023, work-zone accidents on Pennsylvania roads and highways had resulted in 188 deaths. The 22 deaths in 2023 was the highest for a single year on record.[25]

The former Sony plant had earlier been the site of an autonomous vehicle test track. Uber ATG was the first to operate it. Argo AI took it over until the company went out of business. The autonomous trucking company, Stack AV, was next to use it. Uber ATG had also operated a track at Mill 19 in Hazelwood Green for a few years. Neither came close to matching the scale of the PennSTART campus, the master planning for which began in 2023. It was intended for public agencies, universities, and private companies alike. The 100-acre campus was designed with a range of features that autonomous systems would encounter on the outside: stretches of multiple-lane high-speed highways, rural roads, urban streets, intersections with or without traffic signals, a roundabout, gentle loops, tight corners, parking lots, an overhead bridge, highway ramps, railroad crossings, adjustable lighting, and others. It would offer conditions such as rolling hills, flooded areas, potholes, and rough terrain to practice on. Jersey barriers, wrecked vehicles, and other props would be made available, as would rentable autonomous vehicles. All weather conditions would be able to be simulated. There would be a heliport, a place to test aerial drone technologies, charging stations, a range of connectivity options, classrooms, office space, an auditorium, data transmission and storage, and an Innovation Startup Center.[26] "What the industry has learned is that it is going to take a lot more data and testing to get things into the public right of way," said Timothy White, RIDC senior vice president for business development and strategy. "A lot of that is start-ups solving one problem. They need test beds to figure out how to solve the problem on a test site, then maybe move it into an industrial park, which is a semi-public environment, then into the public right of way."

A broader regional strategy for further developing the infrastructure necessary to advance the autonomous systems industry was unfolding around the same time. RIDC and Carnegie Mellon were searching for funds to convert existing public roads and highways into a 39-mile "connected corridor" stretching from Mill 19 in Hazelwood Green—one end of Pittsburgh's Robotics Row—to the PennSTART campus in Westmoreland County. The corridor would be upgraded with technologies that enable autonomous mobile systems to better communicate with one another and the environment around them. Such improvements could range from road markings that are more easily read by the vision systems of self-driving vehicles, to upgrading the entire route with the latest wireless cellular connectivity and technology that sharpens the precision of global positioning systems down to the centimeter.

The path the connected corridor would take from Pittsburgh to Westmoreland remained uncharted in 2024. One route favored by RIDC would loop through the former Mon Valley steel towns, particularly Duquesne and McKeesport, where the two shuttered mills it redeveloped into industrial parks decades earlier had ample room for new tenants and the cities were hungry for jobs and investment. The timeline for the ambitious project was also uncertain, as was whether providing the missing link between the region's autonomous research hub and the state's largest proving ground for those technologies would attract private companies and fuel the industry as hoped. "I don't know which companies are going to succeed, or whether it is going to happen here, but robotics is not going away. Autonomy is not going way. AI is not going away," Smith said in the fall of 2023. "We either bet on it and understand there are going to be wins and losses, or we don't, in which case we know there won't be any wins."

~

RIDC had stabilized its balance sheet, its debt obligations were at a manageable level, and it was no longer cash poor as it moved into the third decade of the 21st century. Revenues in 2023 totaled nearly $40 million, more than 26 times the cash the nonprofit had to work with when it opened its doors in 1955. Rent accounted for all but $1 million of its income. Operating expenses under $30 million and nearly $10 million in debt service left RIDC with a net cash flow of $7 million. It paid nearly $3 million in real estate taxes that year.[27] RIDC had at that point developed upwards of 30 major projects on green suburban acreage and abandoned industrial brownfields into business, research, and light industrial parks. It had built or helped finance hundreds of buildings for established and up-and-coming companies, selling many of them, but keeping 57 under its control. Those it owned housed 118 companies and supported nearly 8,600 jobs.[28]

The most challenging were the steel mills and shuttered factories RIDC acquired during the dark days of the region's manufacturing decline. One exception was Innovation Ridge, a suburban light industrial and research park in Marshall Township north of Pittsburgh. The park remained underwater financially more than a dozen years after RIDC had acquired it and some 25 years after it was first developed as a promising landing spot for technology companies during the heady days of unbridled investment following the birth of the internet. RIDC had taken it over at the request of Allegheny County and the state of Pennsylvania in 2010 when, in the wake of the Great Recession, the foundering park, then called Tech 21, was pushed to the brink of bankruptcy. The county and state—two longtime RIDC partners—stood to lose their considerable investments in the park if it failed. The park's anchor tenant, the medical imaging company Medrad, had left in 2006 after being acquired by Bayer AG. Innovation Ridge struggled to recover despite its proximity to the Pennsylvania Turnpike and Interstate 79. The site had few pads prepared for new construction. More troubling, the downsizing of nearby companies left nearly one million square feet of move-in-ready commercial property available at affordable rates. By 2014, RIDC had decided revising the master plan was necessary to make the site more attractive. "We've learned that the notion of the office park that is just office has fallen out of favor," Smith said. "People want amenities. They want restaurants. They want housing so they can live nearby. The world has changed."

Roughly 25 miles south of Innovation Ridge, RIDC had decided to redevelop another abandoned steel mill in the Mon Valley, the fifth such project the nonprofit had undertaken since the industry collapsed in the 1980s. The Carrie blast furnaces had stood for nearly 140 years along the northern bank of Monongahela River, four miles southeast of the City of Pittsburgh. The furnaces produced as much as 1,250 tons of iron a day that were taken to mills in the Homestead Works down river.[29] The Carrie furnaces had been cold since 1978, when U.S. Steel shut them down. The few still standing were designated a National Historic Landmark. Allegheny County acquired the land from a private developer in 2006 and did environmental remediation, built a fly-over ramp to connect it to the streets of Rankin Borough and asked RIDC to join the project as the developer.

Michael Goldstrom joined RIDC as senior vice president for real estate in 2021, having been recruited from a national commercial real estate firm, a sector in which he had spent more than 20 years of his career after serving as a U.S. Navy officer. He was intrigued by RIDC's public mission of placing economic and community development above profit as the organization's primary concern. "The mission was foreign to me, but it sounded like something that could be very rewarding to be part of," he recalled. "I came into the job knowing I had a lot to learn about economic development and working for a nonprofit and the challenges of the focus on our mission instead of the bottom line, financially—how do we return the most money to investors?—which is what a typical developer looks at." As a private commercial real estate developer, Goldstrom would not have considered the Carrie Furnace site without having a tenant who wanted it and a reliable estimate showing that redeveloping the former steel mill could be done at a cost that would allow for a profit sooner rather than later. "It would be thumbs up or thumbs down

The Carrie Furnaces, originally built in 1884, were acquired by Andrew Carnegie in 1898 and merged into U.S. Steel During its peak, the site produced 1,000 to 1,250 tons of iron per day (top). It ceased production in 1984, with two furnaces remaining as tourism and educational venues and designated as a National Historic Landmark (bottom). Credit for two images above: Rivers of Steel.

In 2022, with those historic furnaces in the background, RIDC entered into an agreement to acquire the 55-acre site and broke ground (top) on a new tech-flex building (bottom)—the first economic activity on the site in 40 years—and announced a partnership with the Pittsburgh Film Office to attract and build a home for a purpose-built film production facility as well.

on whether we could make it pencil. If we couldn't, we'd move on." Building a speculative project at the former mill site with all of the known and unknown risks it presented would've been out of the question.

RIDC broke ground on a speculative "tech-flex" building in 2022 on one portion of the 55-acre site that offered interior spaces that could be modified to suit the changing needs of the technology companies it anticipated attracting. RIDC's plans for a second building catered to a different industry.

Film and television producers for decades had been attracted to southwestern Pennsylvania, where the costs of shooting were relatively low and the topography and diversity of architecture and neighborhoods offered a wide range of locations to meet creative demands. The Pittsburgh skyline had even become Gotham City in *The Dark Knight Rises* installment of the Batman movie franchise. The list of films shot in the region had steadily grown, including Academy Award Best Picture winners *The Deer Hunter* and *Silence of the Lambs*, the Fred Rogers biopic, *A Beautiful Day in the Neighborhood*, the film adaptation of the August Wilson play, *Fences*, and the horror classic, *Night of the Living Dead*. More than 200 movies and television shows had been shot in the region since 1990.[30] More than 42 percent of the film industry jobs in Pennsylvania were in the region. About 41 cents of every dollar filmmakers spent in Pittsburgh flowed to the local supply chain—a spillover rate larger than what two-thirds of local industries generated. Competing against other regions to land more productions meant addressing the local industry's shortcomings. Among them was the lack of a film studio and high-quality production infrastructure, which often left filmmakers to work in converted warehouses scattered about the region with "odd spatial configurations that constrain productions."[31] RIDC hoped to build a studio in the shadow of Carrie Furnace. With the Pittsburgh Film Office as a partner, it set out to create a film campus with purpose-built sound stages and other production facilities long sought by the local industry to further support Pittsburgh's self-assigned reputation as "Hollywood on the Mon." White saw Carrie Furnace as an example of "how partnership and packaging go hand in hand. The plan for a film studio gives the site a focus. Our partnership with the state and county provides resources we need to be successful. That all enabled us to break ground quickly and begin to package the site for prospective tenants."

At the same time, RIDC would bring its experience in brownfield redevelopment to another historic manufacturing plant along a different river in a distressed city 17 miles away that met the nonprofit's criteria as a seedling community.

NEW KENSINGTON

Herb Ray recalled the relief that washed over him when he got a job at the Aluminum Company of America's New Kensington Works, which stretched along the Allegheny River in northern Westmoreland County. His manufacturing experience, which began not long after he graduated from Vandergrift High School in 1951, had been limited to a short stint laboring at a local steel mill, where every workday he had been greeted by knee-buckling heat from the open-hearth furnace and soot-filled air. "It was hell. Not a place where I wanted to spend much time." Alcoa was starkly different. The plant's central machine shop, where he worked

Re:Build Manufacturing executives gave a tour to community leaders of its future home in New Kensington. RIDC acquired the million-square-foot former Alcoa plant in partnership with the Westmoreland County Industrial Development Corporation, with the Re:Build project as centerpiece of a campus-wide revitalization.

until he was transferred to the company's research laboratory eight miles away, was cleaner, safer, better organized and well supervised. And it didn't hurt that Alcoa offered "some of the best-paying jobs in the area." It might not have been heaven, but Ray considered it "the best shop a man could work at."

Alcoa began as the Pittsburgh Reduction Company with an innovative smelting process and a small experimental production plant in the City of Pittsburgh's Strip District in 1888. Three years later, it moved to New Kensington and scaled up to full production of aluminum ingots and a line of cookware, including a popular light but sturdy no-rust teakettle. The plant that was originally 173,000 square feet on 15 acres[32] expanded as decades passed to become a campus with more than one million square feet under roof, spread across nearly 70 acres that employed up to 4,000 workers. Alcoa continued to expand, acquiring numerous companies and establishing operations in nine countries. Lost in the company's rise to international prominence was the New Kensington Works, which Alcoa closed in 1971. Ray, who continued working at the Alcoa research lab, retired in 1993 having spent 40 years with the company.

The City of New Kensington entered a period of gradual decline. By 2022, population had fallen to less than half of what it was at its peak in 1950. The days when the city supported a bustling downtown with several department stores and movie theaters, restaurants and shops, an opera house and its own newspaper had long passed. Nearly 23 percent of its residents were aged 65 years or older. One-third of adults had some college experience or an associate's degree; less than 22 percent had earned a bachelor's or higher degree. Nearly one-fifth of residents lived in poverty. Median household income was $47,000 a year in a county where the average was greater than $71,000.[33]

City government and county economic development officials were working to reverse the caustic trends. Pennsylvania State University, which has a branch campus in New Kensington, chose the city's downtown business district to establish The Corner, which offers services to support entrepreneur and start-up companies. The city, county, and the Richard King Mellon Foundation partnered with the university in 2022 to open The Digital Foundry one block away as a small institute designed to help manufacturers adapt to and compete in a digital business environment and to train workers in technologies they need to master in a rapidly changing workplace. The Digital Foundry was soon chosen as one of the regional centers supported by a federal Build Back Better grant awarded in 2021 to help manufacturing entrepreneurs and small and medium-sized companies adopt advanced robotics and automation technologies. More than 60 new businesses replaced boarded downtown storefronts in short order as part of an initiative to revitalize the "Aluminum City."[34] The plant that gave the city its nickname was seen as an underused asset that could further the cause. The question was, how?

⌒

The former Alcoa plant had been sold to a private developer, which operated it as an industrial district. It attracted a few small companies as tenants, but the rest of the expansive factory complex remained largely unused. Most of the aged buildings were in poor condition.[35] "It had become more of a blight than a benefit to the community," recalled Rigone. The owner was interested in selling. The Westmoreland County Industrial Development Authority, which had been interested in the site for nearly a decade, toured the plant for a closer look. What they found gave them pause. "We were very concerned about its condition on many levels and the capital and human resources that would be necessary to maintain, operate and invest in it," Rigone said. "We had other projects going on in the county. We didn't feel we could take on that risk at the time." The Redevelopment Authority of the City of New Kensington, however, felt the risk was worth taking and bought the plant in 2018, intent on turning it into an attraction for new businesses as part of the city's revitalization campaign. The authority had never undertaken a deteriorated industrial property of such magnitude. It soon became clear that redeveloping and managing the aluminum plant built more a century earlier would stretch its resources beyond their limits.

RIDC, meanwhile, had been "nosing around New Kensington looking for investment opportunities," Smith recalled. The city met the criteria of the nonprofit's seedling program. It was distressed. Local political leadership was investing in meaningful revitalization projects and had attracted influential partners willing to help. "Our investments alone are not going to turn the economic tide for any community. We're not big enough. But if we were able to go in and bring our combination of assessment, market, financial and building capacity to those communities, we could make a material difference in the trajectory of their recovery." What New Kensington lacked were available large-to-medium-scale industrial sites for RIDC to redevelop. "We kicked the tires, but we were having trouble coming up with a plan that worked for us and for them. Just couldn't find the right project."

A phone call changed everything. Kevin Dowling, at the time the chief executive officer of a local mobile autonomy company, Kaarta, informed Smith that an intriguing advanced manufacturing group was scouting locations in the Pittsburgh region for its first ground-up production plant. The group, Re:Build Manufacturing, was chaired by Jeff Wilke, who had spent more than two decades at Amazon, where he was instrumental in making the company a worldwide e-commerce powerhouse as its chief executive of consumer business. Wilke grew up in the Pittsburgh suburb of Greentree and had witnessed the decline of the region's manufacturing base firsthand. Re:Build's lead investor was Thomas Tull, a billionaire businessman, entrepreneur, and film producer who had been chairman and chief executive officer of Legendary Entertainment. He also owned a share of the Pittsburgh Steelers. Re:Build was acquiring a curated network of businesses across the United States to form a contract manufacturing company with a resilient supply chain and the capability to design, engineer, and manufacture products using advanced technologies to lower production costs and compete in the global market for components and finished goods in industries ranging from electric vehicles, energy, aerospace, and medical devices to sports equipment. Re:Build wanted to redevelop a former industrial site for its first production plant, preferably in a community in need of revitalization. What made Re:Build particularly intriguing to RIDC was that the company was attempting to leverage the kind of innovations coming out of local research institutions, such as Carnegie Mellon and the Manufacturing Futures Institute at Hazelwood Green, to modernize American manufacturing. "These were serious people with serious track records who'd raised a serious amount of money and had a vision for restoring industrial jobs and manufacturing in the United States in places where it used to be," Smith recalled. "Those are rare opportunities."

RIDC worked with the Pittsburgh Regional Alliance to put together a list of possible sites, including the former Sony plant in Westmoreland County, and met with company officials to determine what they were looking for in a facility, including what they were looking to pay per square foot to lease. Site visits were arranged. In the end, Re:Build favored the former Alcoa plant, its location, and history. Concerns included the conditions of the buildings in the factory complex and whether the site could be redeveloped to the company's satisfaction without pricing it out of the competition. Re:Build was also looking at industrial sites outside of Pennsylvania, including Ohio locations in Cleveland and Akron.

The Redevelopment Authority of the City of New Kensington had submitted a proposal. RIDC estimated it would require an investment of tens of millions of dollars to bring three buildings for Re:Build up to code and make them usable. Goldstrom found nearly all of the buildings to be in "extremely poor condition." He found evidence that most "had been left without a capital maintenance program of any amount." He estimated that up to 90 percent of the roofs had to be replaced. Much of the electrical infrastructure was "past its usefulness." Several buildings had "no life left in them" and would have to be razed. The New Kensington authority had already acquired more than $10 million in debt to buy the plant. The rent it was charging existing tenants was well below market rate, which made maintaining the plant and paying down the debt difficult. The authority lacked experience with industrial brownfields requiring major redevelopment, which not only required dealing with known challenges, but those unforeseen as well. Re:Build found the authority's proposal unsatisfactory. "When it was clear the deal was going sideways," Smith recalled, "we stepped in."

~

Neither RIDC nor the Westmoreland County Industrial Development Corporation needed to be convinced that recruiting Re:Build had the potential to greatly benefit New Kensington, the neighboring City of Arnold, and southwestern Pennsylvania. Re:Build estimated the plant would create 300 good-paying jobs within a few years and the former Alcoa site offered plenty of room for it to expand, if business warranted. It could buoy local suppliers and demonstrate advanced manufacturing technologies that researchers in Pittsburgh were among the leaders in developing. It was gaining a national reputation as a star among a new wave of innovative manufacturers whose success could attract other companies. It was an organization with an ethos that included workforce development and improving the well-being of the communities around them. But it was not clear whether a deal could be made that would convince Re:Build to choose New Kensington over other competitors without putting RIDC and the Westmoreland agency in financial peril.

The first step was for the two to agree to a partnership. Their partnership at the former Sony plant had been fruitful. Negotiating another for the Alcoa site "was an easy conversation," Rigone recalled. RIDC would hold 51 percent equity in the property and manage redevelopment; Westmoreland would hold 49 percent equity. Next, they acquired the Alcoa site from the Redevelopment Authority of the City of New Kensington in exchange for assuming the authority's $10.7 million debt on the property and named the site the New Kensington Advanced Manufacturing Park. Then began the time-sensitive task of finding the money to finance the redevelopment that would allow them to draft a firm proposal before Re:Build made its decision. The age and condition of the New Kensington site made it challenging. Several other sites Re:Build was considering around the country were newer and in better condition, allowing competitors to offer low-cost lease arrangements. RIDC estimates put the cost of redeveloping the buildings for Re:Build at the Alcoa site at upwards of $28 million.[36] Political contacts were solicited for commitments to put public money into the project. Amounts were negotiated. When gaps arose, other sources of financing were approached—all while the clock was ticking.

~

On the first day of May 2023, Pennsylvania governor Josh Shapiro appeared before an audience of southwestern Pennsylvania political and civic leaders and news reporters at Acrisure Stadium, home of the Pittsburgh Steelers. He had come to make a "major announcement about the future of manufacturing in western Pennsylvania—an investment in our Commonwealth's future that is going to change lives and reshape communities just a few miles up the Allegheny River that have been forgotten for too long."[37] A deal had been reached to bring Re:Build Manufacturing to the New Kensington Advanced Manufacturing Park.

Re:Build would occupy three buildings that collectively offered 175,000 square feet under roof, about 15 percent of the square footage available at the former Alcoa New Kensington Works. Redeveloping the three buildings would cost about $31 million. The state contributed nearly $19 million in grants and low-interest Pennsylvania Industrial Development Authority loans. The Richard King Mellon Foundation contributed $5 million. RIDC and the Westmoreland County Industrial Development Authority each put in roughly $3 million, in addition to assuming more than $10 million in city redevelopment authority debt. Re:Build pledged to invest $50 million in manufacturing equipment and making improvements to fine-tune the buildings to its specific needs.

Jeff Wilke took the podium and recounted how during the COVID-19 pandemic the seeds of what would become Re:Build were sown when he and company chief executive officer Miles Arnone "started talking about all of the failures in our supply chain, which had become so evident to all of us, and ways we might help to change the course of the country." He reported the company had assembled an engineering and technology team that had already grown to more than 400 people across all engineering disciplines, and he predicted the New Kensington plant would become "a beacon of possibility for what the region and country can achieve."[38] Shapiro took advantage of the high-profile event to warn that Pennsylvania in recent years had put itself at a disadvantage by falling behind neighboring states that "devote more resources to economic development, economic incentives that drive the kind of investments we are celebrating here today." Under such circumstances, partnerships and rallying private sector and local government support proved decisive in recruiting Re:Build, which, in turn, had allowed the Commonwealth to "plant a flag showing other states that Pennsylvania is ready to be competitive again."

In the days that followed the announcement, contractors began to descend upon the former Alcoa New Kensington Works, taking up wood-block flooring impregnated with decades of industrial grime, rearranging utilities, insulating, repairing roof, and building interior walls as they reconfigured and rehabilitated the century-old buildings into modern factories for the new tenant. RIDC was back at work, having again bet that a relic of the past could become home to the future.

Inheriting a Legacy, Building a New Future

By Donald F. Smith Jr., President, RIDC

August 2024

When I became president of RIDC 16 years ago, having served on its board of directors and having held the position of economic development lead for both Carnegie Mellon University and the University of Pittsburgh, I was not exactly a newcomer to the organization. I was keenly aware of the legacy I was inheriting from the leaders who'd come before me and of the responsibility with which I was being entrusted—a position that could have an enduring impact on the economic vitality of the southwestern Pennsylvania region.

Seventy years is a long time for an organization to continue to have the kind of impact RIDC has had. It's a tribute to those who founded it: corporate giants who saw a need and had the vision to create an entity that could play a tangible role in diversifying the region's economy. The commitment to that dynamic vision has never wavered. After 70 years, we are still creating spaces and places for economic growth, taking on the most challenging projects, producing tangible results and high-quality jobs for communities and the region as a whole.

From the beginning, RIDC has learned from and responded to the needs of the marketplace and its tenants. When it was clear there was a need for dedicated space for light manufacturing and growing businesses to locate in planned business and industrial parks, RIDC developed the first industrial park in the region, RIDC O'Hara Industrial Park, followed by Thorn Hill and Park West.

RIDC senior vice presidents Mike Goldstrom (left) and Tim White (right) and RIDC president Don Smith (center) tour Mill 19.

When the steel mills and other heavy industries left the region, RIDC started focusing on those sites, including the Pittsburgh Technology Center—which became the template for the PA Land Recycling Law (Act 2)—Keystone Commons, City Center Duquesne, and Industrial Center of McKeesport. The work we did remediating brownfields during this period set the standard and resulted in the environmental remediation statutes that are still in place today.

As our top research universities grew in size and stature and were poised to become major drivers of economic development, RIDC partnered with them to build facilities, including the Collaborative Innovation Center and Software Engineering Institute with Carnegie Mellon University, and the Magee Research Facility with the University of Pittsburgh and UPMC. Projects like these supported the universities' role in the economic ecosystem and were also factors in the attraction to

RIDC president Donald F. Smith Jr. joins Governor Josh Shapiro and Secretary of the Department of Community and Economic Development Rick Siger at an announcement at RIDC's Mill 19 of the governor's economic plan.

our region of companies like Google, Apple, and Disney, which place a high value on the talent the universities provide.

As robotics and life sciences entrepreneurs began to emerge from the universities and needed their own space, RIDC became the developer that, because of our nonprofit status and mission-driven approach, was able to provide more flexibility and accept more risk. At the former Heppenstall Steel site and factory for Geoffrey Boehm chocolates, we created the Lawrenceville Technology Center and built robotics-oriented and life sciences lab space. We also created a new category of real estate with the tech/flex Tech Forge facility—long before the area became known as part of "Robotics Row."

More recently, the need to view southwestern Pennsylvania as a regional economy—setting priorities, allocating resources, and marketing our attributes—has become more evident, as other regions around the country compete aggressively to attract the same job-creating companies. RIDC has responded by entering into partnerships with municipal and county economic development entities on a range of regionally significant projects, ranging from our Westmoreland Innovation Center and New Kensington Advanced Manufacturing Park, to our Armstrong Innovation Center, to our Fairywood development in the City of Pittsburgh.

RIDC has also taken over management of the Strategic Investment Fund (SIF), a private sector source of financing for catalytic projects, originally founded by the Allegheny Conference in 1996. With a new regional approach that could include investments in strategic projects in Pittsburgh and around the 12-county Southwestern Pennsylvania region, SIF has the potential to spark regional economic growth with gap financing for projects that support job creation, community revitalization, and the regional economy overall.

Over the decades, RIDC's board, executive team, and staff have changed and the organization adapted to changing global and local economic issues. Through it all, the vision, mission, and sense of purpose has remained—and the track record of success has grown. As of this writing, RIDC owns nearly 8 million square feet in 57 buildings at 15 locations. Occupying our buildings are 118 companies providing jobs for 8,500 people. And properties we developed and own, many of which had been languishing previously, paid nearly $3 million in local property taxes last year.

Three Ps—partnership, packaging, and patience—have become embedded in our planning and execution of major projects. We partner with local economic development entities that know their communities and can leverage local resources for the benefit of the companies we're trying to attract. The current financing environment—tightened commercial credit and diminished government resources—requires a tremendous amount of financial packaging, connecting the dots and putting myriad pieces together to make a deal work.

And patience is an attribute that makes RIDC truly unique. Unlike for-profit developers, our focus in taking on projects is their potential job-creating impact and tax base enhancement for communities and the region. This can take time. Our strong balance sheet, reputation for getting things done, and commitment to our mission enables us to stick with projects we believe in for as long as it takes.

Partnership also means communicating with stakeholders, including our tenants and other growing businesses in strategically important industries. In addition to informing our development strategy, those relationships enable us to serve as thought leaders and advocates for the public policy initiatives companies need in order to grow.

RIDC's public policy advocacy has been long-standing, from the enactment of Act 2, the environmental remediation legislation that Governor Tom Ridge signed in a ceremony at our Industrial Center of McKeesport in 1995, to the Forefront report we sponsored more recently with the Greater Pittsburgh Chamber of Commerce and the Richard King Mellon Foundation, highlighting the importance of the autonomous technology industry, recommending legislative changes and leading to the PennSTART test track and research facility, which will be located at our Westmoreland Innovation Center.

We also supported plans advanced by Governor Josh Shapiro to create a fund for preparing large sites for the kind of development that attracts major employers who, in turn, can attract employees and new residents. And we are beginning to work with communities around our region that lack some of the expertise and resources necessary to develop assets that have strong economic potential. Our hope is that this "Seedling" initiative can help these communities put together all the elements necessary for success.

I am proud of the role we play in helping our region meet its challenges, and I'm proud that RIDC has earned a reputation as the go-to development organization that gets complex projects done. Our finances are strong, we generate tax revenue for the region and local government entities, and we have a tangible impact on people, places, and the creation of jobs.

I'm proud of the trusted partnerships we've developed and support we've received from the Commonwealth of Pennsylvania, Governor Shapiro, members of the state Legislature, county and local officials around our region, and the foundations that devote tremendous resources to so many important regional initiatives. Without the support of these leaders of our communities, RIDC would not be able to do the work it does.

But I'm particularly proud to be part of our outstanding team—a team that would be sought after by any private developer anywhere. Everyone gets up in the morning and goes to work with a shared mission and they achieve it through skill, commitment, and hard work. It is a group of the best people, all committed to increasing the public good, and it's a privilege to be a part of it.

Whether it involves foreseeable challenges—downtown office building vacancies post-COVID, loss of population in the region, preparing larger sites to attract larger, job-creating companies while also supporting local communities through its Seedling initiative—or challenges that are not yet apparent, RIDC will be at work, identifying opportunities to point the region's economy toward the future and making those visions into reality.

NOTES

Many of the books, newspaper and magazine articles, studies, and other publications this book is drawn from are referenced below. Not referenced are the interviews that proved critical to understanding the evolution of the Regional Industrial Development Corporation and the context in which it occurred. Among those interviewed for this book were Reynolds Clark, Lee Gevaudan, John Bares, Maxwell King, Grant Oliphant, Ray Maffit, Timothy McNulty, Robert Pease, Sam Reiman, Jason Rigone, Frank Brooks Robinson Sr., Michael Goldstrom, Mark Urbassik, Donald Smith, and Timothy White.

INTRODUCTION

1. Statement by the President on G20 Summit in Pittsburgh, September 8, 2009. www.whitehouse.gov/the_press_office/Statement-by-the-President-on-G-20 -Summit-in-Pittsburgh/

2. Remarks by President Barack Obama at G20 Summit closing press conference, David L. Lawrence Convention Center, Pittsburgh, PA, September 25, 2009.

3. Bahr, J., Renaissance: Thriving on diversity instead of its mills. *Financial Times*, September 23, 2009. www.ft.com/cms/s/0/043160d0-a7e4-11de-b0ee -00144feabdc0,s01=1.html

4. Smith, C., Pittsburgh, city of renewal. *The Atlantic*, September 24, 2009. www .theatlantic.com/doc/200909u/g-20-pittsburgh

5. Laneri, R., Pittsburgh? Yes, Pittsburgh. Forbes.com, September 2, 2009. www.forbes.com/2009/09/02/pittsburgh-g-20-economy-innovation-opinions -columnists-21-century-cities-09-pittsburgh.html

6. Lubove, R., *Twentieth Century Pittsburgh, The Post-Steel Era Volume II*, Pittsburgh, PA: University of Pittsburgh Press, 1996, p. ix.

The First Pittsburgh Renaissance

1. Wall, J. F., *Andrew Carnegie*, 2nd ed., University of Pittsburgh Press, Pittsburgh, PA, 1989, p. 386.

2. Lubove, S., *Pittsburgh*, New Viewpoints, New York, 1976.

3. Gugliotta, A., How, when, and for whom was smoke a problem in Pittsburgh, in Tarr, J. A., ed., *Devastation and Renewal*, University of Pittsburgh Press, Pittsburgh, PA, 2003, p. 122.

4. Alberts, R. C., *The Shaping of the Point*, University of Pittsburgh Press, Pittsburgh, PA, 1989, p. 69.

5. Muller, E. K., Downtown Pittsburgh, in Muller, E., and Tarr, J., eds., *Making Industrial Pittsburgh Modern*, University of Pittsburgh Press, Pittsburgh, PA, 2019, p. 415.

6. Mershon, S. R., and Tarr, J. A., Strategies for Cleaner Air, in Tarr, J. A., ed., *Devastation and Renewal*, University of Pittsburgh Press, Pittsburgh, PA, 2003, p. 162.

7. Mershon, Strategies for Cleaner Air, in *Devastation and Renewal*, p. 161.

8. Tarr, J. A., The Cable and Street Car Networks, in Muller et al., eds., *Making Industrial Pittsburgh Modern*, 2019, p. 148.

9. Heinz History Center, The St. Patrick's Day flood of 1936. https://www.heinzhistorycenter.org/blog/western-pennsylvania-history-st-patricks-day-flood-1936/

10. Briem, C., For Pittsburgh a future not reliant on steel was unthinkable . . . and unavoidable, *Pittsburgh Post-Gazette*, Pittsburgh, PA, December 23, 2013.

11. US Department of Commerce, Population characteristics of population of the Pittsburgh, Pa. Standard Metropolitan Area: April 1, 1950, in *1950 Census of the Population*, Bureau of the Census, May 17, 1951.

12. Pennsylvania Economy League, Western Division, *A More Effective Industrial Development Program for the Pittsburgh Region*, report prepared for the Allegheny Conference on Community Development and the Pittsburgh Chamber of Commerce, November 1, 1954, p. 75.

13. Serrin, W., *Homestead, The Glory and Tragedy of an American Steel Town*, Vintage Books, New York, 1993, pp. 243–244.

14. Pennsylvania Economy League, *A More Effective Industrial Development Program for the Pittsburgh Region*, p. 1.

15. Robert C. Stephenson, President's Report, addendum to RIDC board minutes, September 25, 2008.

16. Robin chosen head of industrial plan, *Pittsburgh Press*, July 30, 1955, p. 3.

17. Robin chosen head of industrial plan, *Pittsburgh Press*, July 30, 1955, p. 1.

18. Minutes of RIDC board of directors meeting, August 8, 1955, p. 2.

19. Pennsylvania Economy League, *A More Effective Industrial Development Program for the Pittsburgh Region*, p. 78.

20. Regional Industrial Development Corporation statement of recorded cash receipts and disbursements, August 8, 1955, through August 31, 1956, Price Waterhouse & Co., December 26, 1956.

21. Pennsylvania Economy League, *A More Effective Industrial Development Program for the Pittsburgh Region*, p. 30.

22. Minutes of RIDC board of directors meeting, May 3, 1956.

23. Pennsylvania Economy League, *A More Effective Industrial Development Program for the Pittsburgh Region*, p. 58.

24. Minutes of RIDC board of directors meeting, May 3, 1956.

25. Minutes of RIDC board of directors meeting, July 22, 1958.

26. RIDC press release, in minutes of RIDC board of directors meeting, May 14, 1959.

27. Cabot, Cabot & Forbes. https://ccfne.com/about/

THE WORKHOUSE

1. Minutes of RIDC board of directors meeting, December 3, 1957.

2. MacGregor, D., *Coopers with Conviction: The Allegheny County Workhouse and the Pennsylvania Oil Industry*, Old Western Pennsylvania, April 26, 2020. http://www.oldwesternpa.com/2020/04/coopers-with-conviction-allegheny.html

3. Leslie, A. H., *Fifty-Eighth Annual Report of the Managers of the Allegheny County Workhouse and Inebriate Asylum*, 1927, pp. 89–93. https://archive.org/details/annualreportofma00alle_6/page/n121/mode/2up?view=theater

4. Berkman, A. *Prison Memoirs of an Anarchist*, AK Press: Chico, CA, p. 267.

5. Minutes of executive committee of RIDC board of directors meeting, November 22, 1963.

6. Minutes of executive committee of RIDC board of directors meeting, September 21, 1963.

7. Minutes of executive committee of RIDC board of directors meeting, March 3, 1964.

8. Wade L., Fite: Founder of successful high-tech company while teaching physics at Pitt, *Pittsburgh Post-Gazette*, February 27, 2002. https://old.post-gazette.com/obituaries/20020227fite0227p3.asp

9. Minutes of RIDC board of directors meeting, February 13, 1967.

10. Minutes of RIDC board of directors meeting, July 5, 1967.

11. Minutes of executive committee of RIDC board of directors meeting, March 3, 1964.

12. Hritz, T., Ryan Heads PUTC; Skybus Endorsed, *Pittsburgh Post-Gazette*, October 21, 1969, p. 17.

13. Hanbury, M. R., and Lewes, D. W., *Reston: A Planned Community in Fairfax County, Virginia*, Virginia Department of Historical Resources, 2021, pp. 27–28.

14. Pitz, M., Stanley Hoss: A most wanted man, *Pittsburgh Post-Gazette*, March 18, 2015. https://newsinteractive.post-gazette.com/thedigs/2015/03/18/stanley -hoss-a-most-wanted-man/

15. Minutes of RIDC board of directors meeting, September 20, 1971.

16. Toner, A. J., *Guide to the Thorn Hill School for Boys Records 1909–1962*, Historic Pittsburgh, University of Pittsburgh Library System. https://historicpitts-burgh.org/islandora/object/pitt%3AUS-QQS-mss763/viewer

17. Hamilton, T. J., and Kurtzman, D. H., *The Thorn Hill School of Allegheny County*, A report by the subcommittee of the Youth Service Committee of Allegheny County, p. 31.

18. Pennsylvania Economy League, Western Division, *Survey of Local Institutions for Juvenile Delinquents*, a report prepared for the Board of County Commissioners of Allegheny County, July 1956.

19. Minutes of RIDC board of directors meeting, April 7, 1971.

20. Southwestern Pennsylvania Regional Commission, Total population by municipality in Allegheny County, 1930–2010. https://www.spcregion.org/wp -content/uploads/2019/10/Census-munic-pop-decennial-1930-2010-Allegheny -County.pdf

21. Southwestern Pennsylvania Regional Commission, Total population by municipality in Butler County, 1930–2010. https://www.spcregion.org/wp-content /uploads/2019/10/Census-munic-pop-decennial-1930-2010-Butler-County.pdf

22. Minutes of RIDC board of directors meeting, September 21, 1970.

23. Minutes of RIDC board of directors meeting, September 29, 1975.

24. Minutes of RIDC board of directors meeting, September 29, 1975.

STEEL COLLAPSES AND A TECH CENTER RISES

1. U.S. Census Bureau, decennial census, 1930, 1940, 1980.

2. Briem, C., For Pittsburgh a future not reliant on steel was unthinkable . . . and unavoidable, *Pittsburgh Post-Gazette*, December 23, 2013.

3. University of Pittsburgh University Center for Social and Urban Research, How low has Pittsburgh's unemployment rate ever gone? *Pittsburgh Perspectives*, January 4, 2019.

4. Salpukas, A., U.S. Steel defends past policies, *New York Times*, November 29, 1979, Section D, p. 1.

5. Salpukas, A., U.S. Steel is closing 15 plants, with cut of 13,000 employees, *New York Times*, November 28, 1979, p. 1.

6. Minutes of RIDC board of directors meeting, November 19, 1981.

7. Minutes of RIDC board of directors meeting, November 5, 1979.

8. Minutes of RIDC board of directors meeting, June 19, 1980.

9. Minutes of RIDC board of directors meeting, November 19, 1981.

10. Minutes of RIDC board of directors meeting, November 24, 1982.

11. Tarr, D. G., The steel crisis in the United States and the European Community: Causes and adjustments, in Baldwin, R. E., Hamilton, C. B., and Sapir, A., eds., *Issues in US-EC Trade Relations*, University of Chicago Press, 1988, p. 176.

12. Associated Press, "Music" of a giant steel plant fades in Pennsylvania town, *New York Times*, national edition, section A, p. 19.

13. Roth, M., Homestead Works: Steel lives in its stories, *Pittsburgh Post-Gazette*, July 30, 2006.

14. Serrin, W., *Homestead, The Glory and Tragedy of an American Steel Town*, Vintage Books, New York, 1993, p. 294.

15. Briem, C., Recessions and Pittsburgh, *Pittsburgh Economic Quarterly*, University of Pittsburgh University Center for Social and Urban Research, December 2008, p. 1.

16. Venkatu, V., Rust and renewal: A Pittsburgh retrospective, *Industrial Heartland Series*, Federal Reserve Bank of Cleveland, February 2018, p. 3.

17. Deitrick, S., and Briem, C., Allegheny County Economic Trends, prepared for the Allegheny County comprehensive plan, December 2005, p. 17.

18. Minutes of RIDC board of directors meeting, May 11, 1983.

19. Minutes of RIDC board of directors meeting, June 3, 1982.

20. Minutes of RIDC board of directors meeting, November 13, 1984.

21. Serrin, W., *Homestead, The Glory and Tragedy of an American Steel Town*, Vintage Books, New York, 1993, p. 344.

22. *1984 RIDC Annual Report*, pp. 10–11.

23. Davis, C., Jones and Laughlin steelworks: 130 years of industry / 25 years of archaeology, *The Journal of the Society for Industrial Archaeology* vol. 41, no. 2 (2015), pp. 131–142.

24. Minutes of executive committee of RIDC board of directors meeting, March 29, 1984.

25. Lubove, R., *Twentieth Century Pittsburgh, The Post-Steel Era Volume II*, Pittsburgh, PA: University of Pittsburgh Press, 1996, p. 53.

26. Minutes of RIDC board of directors meeting, November 27, 1985.

27. Lubove, R., *Twentieth Century Pittsburgh, The Post-Steel Era Volume II*, Pittsburgh, PA: University of Pittsburgh Press, 1996, p. 53.

28. *Pittsburgh Technology Center (LTV)*, Western Pennsylvania Brownfields Center case study, Carnegie Mellon University, 2007.

29. *Pittsburgh Technology Center (LTV)*, Western Pennsylvania Brownfields Center case study, Carnegie Mellon University, 2007.

FOCUS ON THE MON VALLEY

1. U.S. Census Bureau, decennial census, 1970, 1990.

2. Murphy, T., RIDC industrial parks turn into unfair competition, *The Pittsburgh Press*, September 9, 1991, p. 17.

3. Pennsylvania Industrial Development Authority Act, May 17 (1956) 1955, P.L. 1609, No. 537.

4. Lubove, R., *Twentieth Century Pittsburgh, The Post-Steel Era Volume II*, Pittsburgh, PA: University of Pittsburgh Press, 1996, pp. 36–37.

5. Lubove, *Twentieth Century Pittsburgh*, p. 37.

6. *Pittsburgh Post-Gazette*, Fine tuning RIDC's role, editorial, September 23, 1991, p. 6.

7. Minutes of RIDC board of directors meeting, November 13, 1991.

8. Minutes of RIDC board of directors meeting, November 13, 1991.

9. Lund, K. C., Inside an American factory: The Westinghouse works in 1904, *Library of Congress Information Bulletin* vol. 56, no. 4, February 24, 1997.

10. Davis, B., KDKA: Broadcasting's pioneer station, Pennsylvania Center for the Book, Pennsylvania State University Libraries, University Park, PA, Fall 2010.

11. Minutes of executive committee of RIDC board of directors meeting, August 25, 1987.

12. Minutes of RIDC board of directors meeting, November 11, 1988.

13. Vancheri, B., The sounds of silence, *Pittsburgh Post-Gazette*, March 8, 1991, p. 38.

14. Minutes of RIDC board of directors meeting, November 18, 1992.

15. Minutes of RIDC board of directors meeting, May 13, 1992.

16. Minutes of executive committee of RIDC board of directors meeting, July 6, 1992.

17. Minutes of executive committee of RIDC board of directors meeting, May 12, 1993.

18. Minutes of RIDC board of directors meeting, May 11, 1994.

19. Minutes of RIDC board of directors meeting, November 18, 1998.

20. Fitzpatrick, D., Understanding the Regional Industrial Development Corp., *Pittsburgh Post-Gazette*, August 22, 1999.

21. Barnes, T., RIDC chief criticizes DER staff attitudes, *Pittsburgh Post-Gazette*, April 15, 1993, section B, p. 4.

22. Pennsylvania Land Recycling and Environmental Remediation Standards Act of May 19, 1995, P.L. 4, No. 2Cl. 27, Section 102.

23. Constitution of the Commonwealth of Pennsylvania, Article 1, section 27, added in 1971.

24. Pennsylvania Land Recycling and Environmental Remediation Standards Act of May 19, 1995, P.L. 4, No. 2Cl. 27, Section 501.

25. Minutes of executive committee of RIDC board of directors meeting, February 7, 1990.

26. U.S. Bureau of Labor Statistics, *Producer Price Index by Commodity: Metals and Metal Products: Iron and Steel Scrap* [WPU1012]. https://fred.stlouisfed.org/series/WPU1012

27. Minutes of RIDC board of directors meeting, May 11, 1994.

28. Serrin, W., *Homestead, The Glory and Tragedy of an American Steel Town*, Vintage Books, New York, 1993, p. 355.

29. Briem, C., Voices: Dorothy, revisited, *The Postindustrial*, September 13, 2022. https://postindustrial.com/stories/dorothy-revisited/

30. Greater Pittsburgh Community Food Bank website. https://pittsburgh-foodbank.org/

31. Pennsylvania Turnpike Commission, PA Route 51 to I-376 of the Mon/Valley Expressway. https://www.paturnpike.com/traveling/construction/site/pa-route-51-to-i-376-of-the-mon-fayette-expressway

32. Fitzpatrick, D., Understanding the Regional Industrial Development Corp., *Pittsburgh Post-Gazette*, August 22, 1999.

UNIVERSITY STRATEGY TAKES HOLD

1. Fuoco, M. A., Give up on steel, planners tell towns, *Pittsburgh Post-Gazette*, February 29, 1988, p. 8.

2. Minutes of RIDC board of directors meeting, March 3, 1964.

3. Lubove, R., *Twentieth Century Pittsburgh, The Post-Steel Era Volume II*, Pittsburgh, PA: University of Pittsburgh Press, 1996, p. 43.

4. Fraser, J., Science's role grows in area economy, *The Pittsburgh Press*, September 22, 1985, p. D18.

5. *Strategy 21, Pittsburgh/Allegheny Economic Development Strategy to Begin the 21st Century*, a proposal to the Commonwealth of Pennsylvania, June 1985.

6. Minutes of RIDC board of directors meeting, November 13, 1984.

7. Fraser, J., Heavy demand to use supercomputers blocking access for many scientists, *The Pittsburgh Press*, December 6, 1984, p. 6.

8. McKay, J., Jubilant CMU sees big boost for region, *The Pittsburgh Post-Gazette*, November 15, 1984, p. 1.

9. Fraser, J., CMU signs $103 million high-tech pact, *The Pittsburgh Press*, January 3, 1985, p. 1.

10. Gradek, B., *The Root of Pittsburgh's Population Drain*, Carnegie Mellon University, Center for Economic Development, November 2003, pp. 1–3.

11. Remarks from Timothy Parks were made in a July 3, 2012, interview for a *Pittsburgh Today* report that accompanied a survey of young adults in southwestern Pennsylvania.

12. CMU, city to go beyond education, Cyert says, *Pittsburgh Post-Gazette*, December 2, 1985, p. 9.

13. U.S. Department of Health and Human Services, National Institutes of Health awards by location and organizations.

14. Deitrick, S., Hansen, S. B., and Briem, C., *Gender Wage Disparity in the Pittsburgh Region: Analyzing Causes and Differences in the Gender Wage Gap*, University Center for Social and Urban Research, University of Pittsburgh, December 2007, p. 8.

15. Fee, K., Population distribution and educational attainment within MSAs, 1980–2010, *Economic Commentary*, Federal Reserve Bank of Cleveland, No. 2013-18, November 19, 2013.

16. *Strategy 21, Pittsburgh/Allegheny Economic Development Strategy to Begin the 21st Century*, a proposal to the Commonwealth of Pennsylvania, June 1985, p. 3A.

17. Minutes of the RIDC board of directors meeting, November 18, 1992.

MILL 19

1. Minutes of RIDC board of directors meeting, November 15, 2000.

2. Lubove, R., *Twentieth Century Pittsburgh, The Post-Steel Era Volume II*, Pittsburgh, PA: University of Pittsburgh Press, 1996, p. 105.

3. Minutes of RIDC board of directors meeting, August 9, 1995.

4. Pittsburgh Downtown Partnership, *2020 State of Downtown Pittsburgh: Residential Market Report*.

5. Minutes of RIDC board of directors meeting, September 23, 2003.

6. Minutes of RIDC board of directors meeting, March 26, 2008.

7. Minutes of RIDC board of directors meeting, December 20, 2004.

8. Minutes of RIDC board of directors meeting, April 2, 2009.

9. Minutes of RIDC board of directors meeting, March 26, 2008.

10. Minutes of RIDC board of directors meeting, June 26, 2008.

11. Minutes of RIDC board of directors meeting, March 26, 2008.

12. Fraser, J., Act II: After the mill, *h Magazine*, issue 2 (2012), p. 12

13. Fraser, J., Act II: After the mill, *h Magazine*, issue 2 (2012), p. 17.

14. Schmitz, J., Mon-Fayette road project slowed by lack of funds. *Pittsburgh Post-Gazette*, July 17, 2011. www.post-gazette.com/stories/news/transportation/mon-fayette-road-project-slowed-by-lack-of-funds-306442/

15. Smith, D., RIDC President's Report, December 2013, p. 1.

16. Hazelwood history: Industrial expansion driving out old-fashioned homesteads, *The Pittsburg Leader*, January 27, 1901.

17. Carnegie Library of Pittsburgh, Hazelwood: History. http://www.clpgh.org/exhibit/neighborhoods/hazelwood/haze_n4.html

18. The Hazelwood Neighborhood, 2010, Program in Urban and Regional Analysis, University of Pittsburgh University Center for Social and Urban Research, February 2012. https://www.ucsur.pitt.edu/files/center/Hazelwood%20Neighborhood%20Profile%202010.pdf

19. Fraser, J., Act II: After the mill, *h Magazine*, issue 2 (2012), p. 17.

20. Fraser, J., Easing dividing lines, *h Magazine*, issue 1 (2019), p. 26.

21. Minutes of RIDC board of directors meeting, May 8, 2014.

22. Minutes of RIDC board of directors meeting, January 28, 2015.

23. Minutes of RIDC board of directors meeting, May 8, 2014.

24. Minutes of RIDC board of directors meeting, December 16, 2015.

25. American Institute of Architects, COTE Top 10 Awards, RIDC Mill 19: Buildings A & B, April 20, 2023. https://www.aia.org/design-excellence/award -winners/ridc-mill-19-buildings-b

26. Robinson-Johnson, E., Robotaxi maker Motional, testing its vehicles in Pittsburgh, "not going anywhere," after major investor pulls out, *Pittsburgh Post-Gazette*, February 26, 2024.

27. Fraser, J., From rust to renewal, *h Magazine*, issue 1 (2022), p. 11.

ROBOTICS ROW

1. University of Pittsburgh University Center for Social and Urban Research, *An Atlas of the Lawrenceville Neighborhood of Pittsburgh*, University of Pittsburgh, 1977, p. 2.

2. Paris, B., Song of Lawrenceville, *Pittsburgh Quarterly*, Spring issue, February 2007.

3. Fourth Economy Consulting, *Robots in the backyard: How the National Robotics Engineering Center changed a neighborhood, a region and an industry: An economic impact study*, commissioned by Carnegie Mellon University, December 2021, pp. 9–11.

4. TEConomy Partners, *FOREFRONT: Securing Pittsburgh's Break-out Position in Autonomous Mobile Systems*, report prepared for the Regional Industrial Development Corporation and the Greater Pittsburgh Chamber of Commerce, September 2021, pp. 3–5.

5. Ibid., p. 19.

6. Minutes of RIDC board of directors meeting, September 25, 1995.

7. Minutes of RIDC board of directors meeting, September 25, 1995.

8. Minutes of RIDC board of directors meeting, Lawrenceville Technology Center update, September 20, 2017.

9. Minutes of RIDC board of directors meeting, August 14, 2002.

10. Istrate, E., and Nadeau, C. A., *Global Metro Monitor 2012: Slowdown, Recovery and Interdependence*, Metropolitan Policy Program at Brookings, Brookings Institution, Washington, DC, p. 25.

11. Economic Transformation, in Pittsburgh Today and Tomorrow, *Pittsburgh Quarterly*, Spring 2013, p. 4.

12. Minutes of RIDC board of directors meeting, February 20, 2013.

13. Minutes of RIDC board of directors meeting, May 8, 2014, Historic trends over the last 15 years, PowerPoint presentation, p. 9.

14. Minutes of RIDC board of directors meeting, December 2013.

15. Bishop, T., Why is GeekWire in Pittsburgh? Here is the story behind all of these stories you've been seeing lately. GeekWire, February 5, 2018. https://www .geekwire.com/2018/geekwire-pittsburgh-heres-story-behind-stories-youve-seeing -lately/

16. Minutes of RIDC board of directors meeting, September 20, 2017.

17. Levy, N., Our robotic neighbors: Hanging out with the mechanical inhabitants of "Robotics Row," GeekWire, February 21, 2018. https://www.geekwire.com /2018/robot-neighbors-hanging-helpful-horrifying-inhabitants-robotics-row/

18. Spice, B., and Watzman, A., Carnegie Mellon Tartan Racing wins $2 million DARPA Urban Challenge, Carnegie Mellon University, press release, November 4, 2007.

19. Lassa, T., Level 4 autonomy is dead to Ford—for now, *Autoweek*, October 27, 2022.

20. Thadani, T., Ready or not, self-driving semi-trucks are coming to America's highways, *Washington Post*, March 31, 2024.

21. University of Pittsburgh University Center for Social and Urban Research, Who Moves to Lawrenceville and Why? University of Pittsburgh, May 2012, p. 10.

22. University of Pittsburgh University Center for Social and Urban Research, Who Moves to Lawrenceville and Why? University of Pittsburgh, May 2012, p. 10.

23. Lawrenceville United, *Housing for All*, September 28, 2018.

24. University of Pittsburgh University Center for Social and Urban Research, Who Moves to Lawrenceville and Why? University of Pittsburgh, May 2012, p. 10.

25. Deto, R., Lawrenceville is one of the nation's fastest growing millennial neighborhoods, *Pittsburgh City Paper*, September 19, 2018.

26. Thrush, G., The robots that saved Pittsburgh: How the Steel City avoided Detroit's fate, Politico, February 4, 2014. https://www.politico.com/magazine/story /2014/02/pittsburgh-robots-technology-103062/

27. TEConomy Partners, *FOREFRONT: Securing Pittsburgh's Break-out Position in Autonomous Mobile Systems*, report prepared for the Regional Industrial Development Corporation and the Greater Pittsburgh Chamber of Commerce, September 2021, p. 8.

28. TEConomy Partners, *FOREFRONT: Securing Pittsburgh's Break-out Position in Autonomous Mobile Systems*, report prepared for the Regional Industrial Development Corporation and the Greater Pittsburgh Chamber of Commerce, September 2021, P ES-11.

29. U.S. Economic Development Administration, *FY 2021 EDA American Rescue Plan Act Build Back Better Regional Challenge Notice of Funding Opportunity*, U.S. Department of Commerce, July 22, 2021.

TRULY REGIONAL

1. Farm area to get plant of Chrysler, *New York Times*, September 29, 1968, Section F, p. 17.

2. Boselovic, L., Sony's the 3rd company to fall short in New Stanton, *Pittsburgh-Post Gazette*, March 16, 2007.

3. Acton, R., Workers recall East Huntingdon plant closing, *Tribune-Review*, August 24, 2008.

4. Westmoreland County Industrial Development Corporation, RIDC Westmoreland, a timeline, History of the New Stanton site. https://www.co .westmoreland.pa.us/1494/Project-History

5. Holusha, J., Volkswagen to shut U.S. plant, *New York Times*, November 21, 1987, Section 1, p. 1 of the national edition.

6. Fraser, J., and Ranii, D., Sony's eye is on expansion, *The Pittsburgh Press*, April 18, 1990, p. 1.

7. Minutes of RIDC board of directors meeting, November 8, 1989.

8. Minutes of RIDC board of directors meeting, May 31, 1979.

9. Boselovic, L., Sony's the 3rd company to fall short in New Stanton, *Pittsburgh-Post Gazette*, March 16, 2007.

10. Williams, M., Sony to close last U.S. TV factory, Computerworld, December 10, 2008.

11. Minutes of RIDC board of directors meeting, July 1, 2009.

12. Minutes of RIDC board of directors meeting, January 16, 2010.

13. Minutes of RIDC board of directors meeting, May 19, 2010.

14. Minutes of RIDC board of directors meeting, February 29, 2012.

15. Shapiro, J., Speech delivered in Pittsburgh by Pennsylvania governor Josh Shapiro announcing the redevelopment of the New Kensington Advanced Manufacturing Park, May 1, 2023.

16. Minutes of RIDC board of directors meeting, August 28, 2014.

17. Minutes of RIDC board of directors meeting, March 16, 2016.

18. Minutes of RIDC board of directors meeting, February 29, 2012.

19. Minutes of RIDC board of directors meeting, May 19, 2010.

20. Minutes of RIDC board of directors meeting, February 20, 2013.

21. Minutes of RIDC board of directors meeting, January 22, 2014.

22. Minutes of RIDC board of directors meeting, May 8, 2022.

23. TEConomy Partners, *FOREFRONT: Securing Pittsburgh's Break-out Position in Autonomous Mobile Systems*, report prepared for the Regional Industrial Development Corporation and the Greater Pittsburgh Chamber of Commerce, September 2021, pp. 56–58.

24. Minutes of RIDC board of directors meeting, May 24, 2022.

25. Vendel, C., "These workers deserved to come home": 3 killed on I-83 during National Work Zone Awareness Week, *PennLive*, April 17, 2024.

26. RIDC, *PennSTART and the Connected Corridor*, PowerPoint presentation, November 20, 2023.

27. Minutes of RIDC board of directors meeting, December 13, 2022.

28. RIDC, *RIDC's Mission and History*, February 15, 2023.

29. Carnegie Mellon University, *Carrie Furnace*, Western Pennsylvania Brownfields Center case study, Pittsburgh Carnegie Mellon University, updated 2013.

30. Sciullo, M., How Pittsburgh really will be Hollywood on the Mon in a couple of years, *Pittsburgh Magazine*, March 16, 2023.

31. Peet, E. D., Phillips, B., Walsh, S. J., Steiner, E. D., and Zaber, M. A., *The Film Industry in Pittsburgh, Pennsylvania: Economic Contribution and Capacity for Growth*, Santa Monica, CA, RAND Corporation, 2023.

32. Alcoa—New Kensington Works, *Historic American Engineering Record*, Washington, DC, National Parks Service, Department of the Interior, HAER No. PA-337, p. 1.

33. U.S. Census Bureau, 2022 American Community Survey 5-year estimates.

34. Rittmeyer, B. C., Dignitaries celebrate opening of Digital Foundry in New Kensington, *Tribune Review*, June 1, 2022.

35. Alcoa—New Kensington Works, *Historic American Engineering Record*, Washington, DC, National Parks Service, Department of the Interior, HAER No. PA-337, p. 3.

36. Minutes of RIDC board of directors meeting, December 13, 2022.

37. From remarks made by Pennsylvania governor Josh Shapiro at press conference announcing the redevelopment of the New Kensington Advanced Manufacturing Park, Acrisure Stadium, May 1, 2023.

38. From remarks made by Jeff Wilke during the press conference announcing the redevelopment of the New Kensington Advanced Manufacturing Park, Acrisure Stadium, May 1, 2023.

ABOUT THE AUTHOR

Jeffery Fraser is an award-winning newspaper and magazine journalist in southwestern Pennsylvania. During a career that spanned five decades, he covered a wide range of issues that impact life within the region, from public safety, local government, and the courts to science and medicine, environmental concerns, and economic development. He began work on this book in 2023 after retiring as senior editor of *Pittsburgh Today*, a regional data and journalism program at the University of Pittsburgh Center for Social and Urban Research.

www.ingramcontent.com/pod-product-compliance
Lightning Source LLC
Chambersburg PA
CBHW070332130325
23365CB00005B/13